I0821021

this journal
belongs to

....

THE SELF-CARE DEVOTIONAL *journal*

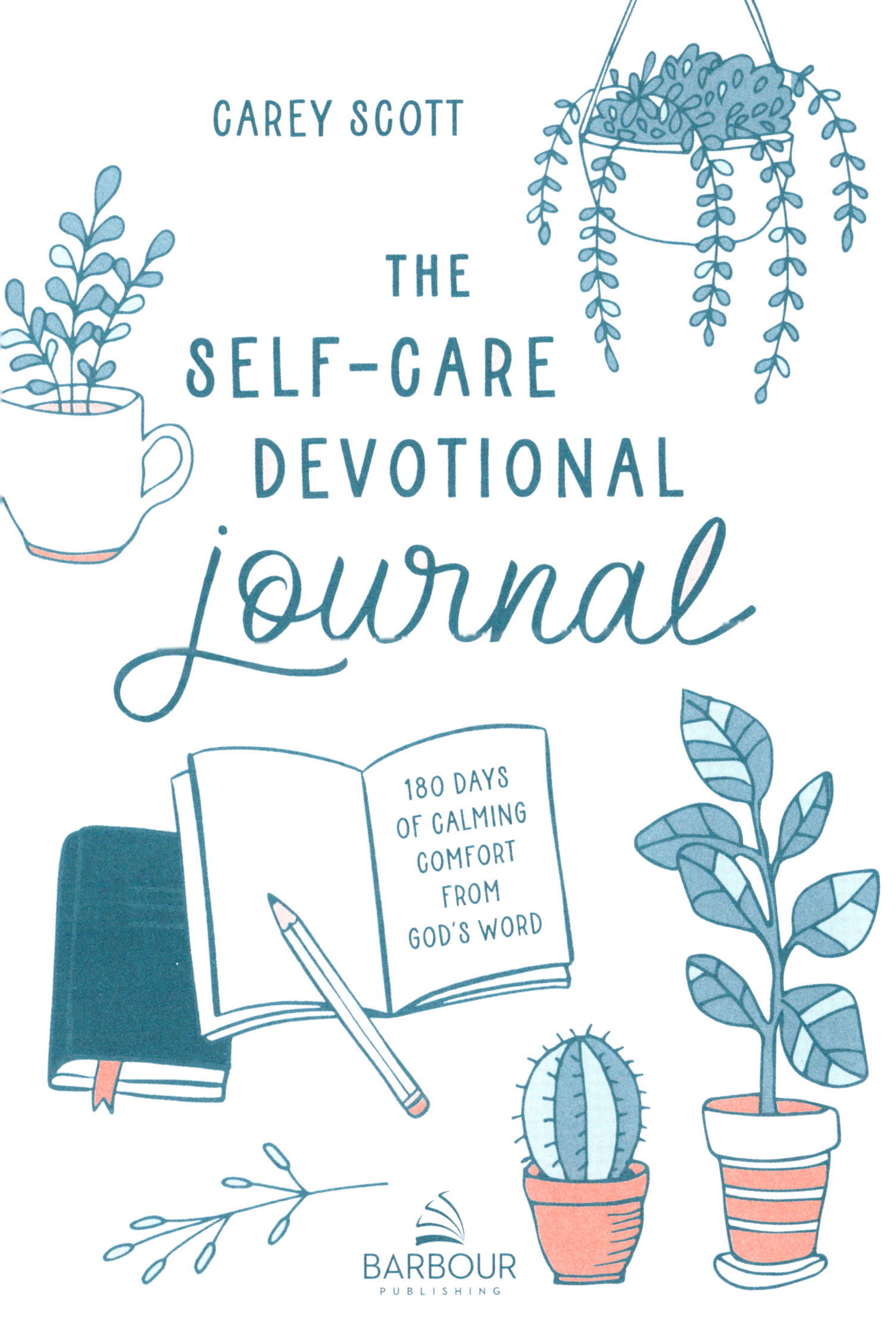
CAREY SCOTT
THE
SELF-CARE
DEVOTIONAL
journal
180 DAYS
OF CALMING
COMFORT
FROM
GOD'S WORD
BARBOUR
PUBLISHING

Print ISBN 979-8-89151-231-3

Cover design: Greg Jackson, Thinkpen Design

Published by Barbour Publishing, Inc., 1810 Barbour Drive, Uhrichsville, Ohio 44683, www.barbourbooks.com

Our mission is to inspire the world with the life-changing message of the Bible.

Printed in China.

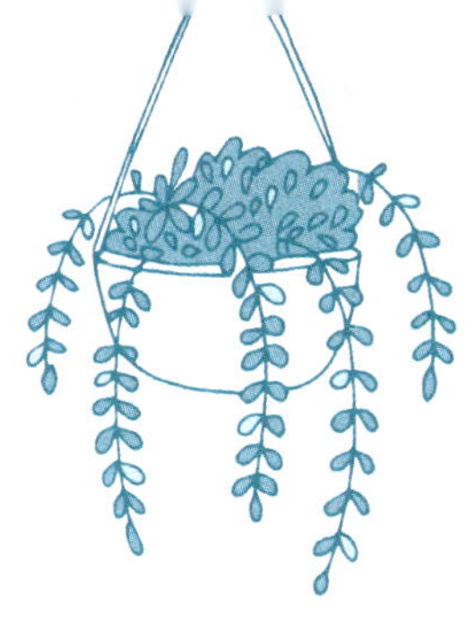

INTRODUCTION

God wants us to care about and invest in our emotional, mental, physical, and spiritual health. Because it's important to Him, it should be important to us too. But don't confuse self-care with self-centeredness. It's not about pushing others aside to make sure your needs are met. It's not an excuse to ignore family and friends, choosing yourself first. Instead, it's about embracing God's plan for your life and learning healthy habits so you can effectively be a light in the world. The pursuit of a healthy *you* is essential so you can love others well. Perfection isn't the goal, but living with passion and purpose is.

Let God speak to you through the pages of this journal, helping you find the right balance in every area of life. Let Him help you prioritize each day so you're set up for His rich blessings. Invite Him into your plans and ideas, expectant for the Lord's goodness to strengthen you for what's ahead. And then watch as you find joy, rest, and peace in His presence. Trusting God in these ways will provide a much-needed stability to your body, soul, and mind. Friend, there is no earthly self-care routine that comes close to a God-care reality.

REASONS TO CARE ABOUT YOURSELF

Dear friend, I'm praying that all is well with you and that you enjoy good health in the same way that you prosper spiritually.

3 JOHN 2 CEB

As you begin this book today, recognize that the goal is for you to find reasons and ways to care for yourself. As women, we're most often the caretakers. We're the ones who make sure everyone else is happy and healthy. And rarely do we take the time to inventory our own heart to see its condition. We overlook our needs and put ourselves second—or tenth. But that isn't God's plan for you.

Understand that your Father cares deeply about you and wants you to take the right steps to stay emotionally, physically, and spiritually healthy. He wants your soul to be well so you can love others from wholesome places. He wants to nourish your spirit and bring you into alignment with His will. And when you slow down, take a deep breath, and spend time with the Lord, He will bless you in wonderful ways. He will heal the broken places. He will bring comfort and hope.

Dear God, remind me to be kind to myself. I'm unable to handle everything on my own. I can't fix everyone's difficult situations. And while I'm to have a servant's heart, I need to care for myself too. Help me find balance. Amen.

THE HOLY SPIRIT'S HOME

Haven't you yet learned that your body is the home of the Holy Spirit God gave you, and that he lives within you? Your own body does not belong to you. For God has bought you with a great price. So use every part of your body to give glory back to God because he owns it.

1 CORINTHIANS 6:19–20 TLB

If God wants us to use every part of our bodies to give glory, then we need to be kinder to ourselves. We need to get quality sleep each night. We need to move our bodies regularly so we stay fit. We need to be mindful about the food we eat and what we drink, making sure we're getting the right nourishment. And we need to feed our spirits on God's Word. Why? Because the Holy Spirit lives in us, it's crucial we take care of His home.

Knowing this, what are some changes you should make? Where can you be more mindful of your body's needs? How can you honor the Lord by caring for yourself inside and out? Friend, don't underestimate the value of self-care.

Dear God, thank You for reminding me that my body houses Your Holy Spirit. What an honor to have Your presence within me. Help me take care of myself so He has a happy and holy place to dwell. Amen.

FINDING REST

So there is a full complete rest still waiting for the people of God. Christ has already entered there. He is resting from his work, just as God did after the creation. Let us do our best to go into that place of rest, too, being careful not to disobey God as the children of Israel did, thus failing to get in.

HEBREWS 4:9–11 TLB

Rest. What a challenging concept to understand and an even harder one to walk out. Do you ever wonder just when you could find the time to do so? Most of us hit the ground running once our alarm wakes us up. We immediately go into warp speed as we try to get everyone fed and out the door. If we aren't going to the office, we're trying to tackle our long to-do list. And we end our day by falling into bed after cooking and cleaning for those we love, only to do it again tomorrow.

But consider that we can rest even amid our busyness. While grocery shopping, carpooling, working, and managing multiple schedules, our spirit can rest in God's goodness until our body can rest from the hustle and bustle. Ask God to show you how to embrace His rest, regardless of what you're doing.

Dear God, show me what rest looks like as I tackle my day. Help me find a peaceful place regardless of my calendar. Teach me to rest. Amen.

PRAY INSTEAD OF WORRY

Don't fret or worry. Instead of worrying, pray. Let petitions and praises shape your worries into prayers, letting God know your concerns. Before you know it, a sense of God's wholeness, everything coming together for good, will come and settle you down. It's wonderful what happens when Christ displaces worry at the center of your life.

PHILIPPIANS 4:6–7 MSG

Rather than letting frustrations build up, go right to God with every concern. When you're feeling the effects of stress in your body—manifesting as sleepless nights and restless days—let petitions shape your worries into prayers. The reality is there's nothing good or productive about an anxious heart, and God can replace it with peace.

Part of caring for yourself is knowing when it's time to place every burden at the Father's feet. Share your frustrations in marriage. Unpack your fears in parenting. Tell God why you feel stuck. When you do, His presence will settle you down. Something supernatural will happen, and you'll feel hope rise up. And before you know it, God's comfort will cover your heart and bring much-needed rest and joy.

Dear God, I'm coming to You with the heavy worries that are bogging me down. I feel the weight of them on my chest. Please take them from me so I can breathe. Exchange them for Your perfect peace. Amen.

YOU ARE THE TEMPLE OF GOD

You realize, don't you, that you are the temple of God, and God himself is present in you? No one will get by with vandalizing God's temple, you can be sure of that. God's temple is sacred—and you, remember, are the temple.

1 CORINTHIANS 3:16–17 MSG

When scripture says, "No one will get by with vandalizing God's temple," consider that also includes you. The Lord wants us to be intentional about caring for ourselves, as we may be the only ones who do. And if we are reckless with the bodies we've been given, realize we are damaging the Spirit's temple too.

The goal isn't to be overconcerned and selfish. God is clear that we're to love others as we love ourselves. But we are called to steward these bodies well. If we don't, we'll be unable to walk out the calling placed on our lives. We won't have the energy to serve those around us. And we may eventually shut down because we didn't heed our bodies' warning signs.

Friend, you are the temple of God. Ask Him to help you protect yourself, honoring the home where He has chosen to dwell.

Dear God, what a privilege to house Your Holy Spirit in my heart. Help me make choices that will keep me happy and healthy and also bless You at the same time. Amen.

RESTORING RELATIONSHIPS

And now I want to plead with those two dear women, Euodias and Syntyche. Please, please, with the Lord's help, quarrel no more—be friends again.

PHILIPPIANS 4:2 TLB

We've all had fights with friends and family members. We have had to navigate the inevitable ups and downs that come with relationships, feeling the stress those can often bring. But it's important to our well-being and overall mental health that we find the path to peace. Community is a beautiful tool God created for believers.

Don't overlook the help God will give to those who ask. Are you struggling to forgive someone or to ask for their forgiveness? Are you lacking the gumption to reach out and work toward restoration? Are you having a hard time understanding their feelings as well as your own? Let God guide your heart toward reconciliation. Part of self-care is allowing others to support us through life. We need community in both the good and the bad times.

Dear God, thank You for the gift of community. I confess the times I've taken it for granted, being reckless with those I care about the most. Help me keep short accounts of wrongs so my relationships remain healthy. And remind me of the many benefits that come from being surrounded by wonderful and supportive friends and family. Amen.

REJOICE IN THE LORD

Most of all, friends, always rejoice in the Lord! I never tire of saying it: Rejoice! Keep your gentle nature so that all people will know what it looks like to walk in His footsteps. The Lord is ever present with us.

PHILIPPIANS 4:4–5 VOICE

Taking the time and making the effort to find joy in God's goodness helps you stay emotionally balanced. Life is hard, and struggles are part of the journey. We will have difficult days and painful seasons. We'll experience heartache on epic levels more than once. And we will have times when we will want to crawl into bed and pull the covers up over our heads. But as a believer, there is always something to be joyful about.

In those tough moments, why not journal about times You saw God show up? Let your mind revisit occasions when you felt His presence overwhelm you with peace and comfort. Think about instances when your steps of faith were rewarded with gracious blessings. And, friend, rejoice in the Lord, for He is a good, good Father!

Dear God, let me always rejoice in Your goodness, knowing it will feed my soul and settle my spirit. Help me keep a posture of praise when my body wants to shut down. You are the only one who can restore me. Amen.

YOUR THOUGHTS MATTER

Finally, brothers and sisters, fill your minds with beauty and truth. Meditate on whatever is honorable, whatever is right, whatever is pure, whatever is lovely, whatever is good, whatever is virtuous and praiseworthy.
PHILIPPIANS 4:8 VOICE

One of the most important ways you can care for yourself is by taking every negative thought captive. We can be so hard on ourselves. Our self-talk can be intense and brutal. But when we intentionally fill our minds with beauty and truth, it helps our hearts to remain hopeful. Rather than get pulled down by pessimism, we have the opportunity to redirect our thoughts.

Friend, meditate on things that are decent and worthy. Think on whatever is right and pure. Choose to concentrate on what is lovely. What is good in your life? Focus on these with passion. Give your attention to what is moral or virtuous. And be deliberate to chew on things praiseworthy. If you keep your thoughts on the path of righteousness, your heart will follow. And your soul will be nourished.

Dear God, I confess how easy it is for my mind to wander into negativity. When it does, it affects how I feel and what I do. Help me protect my thoughts. Help me meditate on Your goodness so my soul is at peace. Amen.

THRIVING IN GOD'S POWER

I know how to live on almost nothing or with everything. I have learned the secret of contentment in every situation, whether it be a full stomach or hunger, plenty or want; for I can do everything God asks me to with the help of Christ who gives me the strength and power.

PHILIPPIANS 4:12–13 TLB

Let today's verse challenge you to rest in the Lord. As women, we're constantly pulled in a million different directions. From sunup to sundown, too often our calendars are sheer insanity. We may be able to multitask with the best of them, but that's not a healthy pace. And constantly working to keep up with others and trying to please everyone breeds discontentment. We're just too aware of where we're falling short.

But when we change our focus from striving in our own strength to thriving in God's power, we'll be able to catch our breath and experience comfort. The rat race won't trap us any longer. We won't feel as if we need to hit the ground running. And trusting God for our needs will calm our anxious hearts and lighten our emotional loads.

Dear God, help me find contentment as I trust You to provide everything I need. I don't need to strive, because when I put faith in You, I will thrive. Amen.

GOD WILL SUPPLY

And my God will liberally supply (fill until full) your every need according to His riches in glory in Christ Jesus.

PHILIPPIANS 4:19 AMP

When you feel depleted and lacking, talk to your Father in heaven. There's no reason to look to earthly solutions to meet your basic or complex needs, because what they can offer you isn't long lasting. You don't need to dig deep to muster the strength to handle things yourself. And if you're looking for a worldly resolution, you will not find one. Scripture is clear that it's God alone who will supply your every need. Even more, He will do so liberally.

Part of self-care includes knowing when to surrender to the Lord, choosing to trust His plans for your life. It requires understanding your human limitations and acknowledging that God is God and you are not. And when you flex your faith, trusting He knows what is best for you in that moment, you will be blessed.

Dear God, every time I look to the world for relief, please remind me that You alone are my source. My friends and family may try to support me, but Your track record in doing so is perfect. You promise to meet my every need liberally. And I know Your promises are never broken. Thank You for being that kind of Father. Amen.

THE BEAUTY OF SPEAKING UP

Brothers, if anyone is caught in any sin, you who are spiritual [that is, you who are responsive to the guidance of the Spirit] are to restore such a person in a spirit of gentleness [not with a sense of superiority or self-righteousness], keeping a watchful eye on yourself, so that you are not tempted as well.

GALATIANS 6:1 AMP

Sometimes God uses people to speak hard truths into our lives. Hearing criticism is not easy, even if under the guise of being constructive. No one enjoys being told the raw truth, even if done through the lens of love. The reality is we don't always want others to be all up in our business. But, friend, when we're heading in the wrong direction and someone cares enough to speak up, embrace it.

When we're overwhelmed and ignoring all our internal warning signs, it's often because we're not prioritizing self-care. We may choose to overlook our needs as we make sure everyone else is doing okay first. We have children and husbands, careers and aging parents, volunteer work and friendships, and there are times we fall to the bottom of the list. Ask God to surround you with solid people who will speak up when needed and for a heart to hear them when they do.

Dear God, when someone comes to me with honest concerns, help me embrace their words and listen with humility. Amen.

SHARING ONE ANOTHER'S TROUBLES

Share each other's troubles and problems, and so obey our Lord's command. If anyone thinks he is too great to stoop to this, he is fooling himself. He is really a nobody.

GALATIANS 6:2–3 TLB

Is it hard for you to accept help? For many, being able to admit we're struggling to effectively handle certain circumstances on our own is challenging because it makes us feel weak. It makes us feel incapable of adulting. So rather than reaching out to trusted friends and family, we work overtime to fix things ourselves. Sound familiar?

When God created community, He did so knowing we'd need one another. His plan was never for us to be alone, which the Lord confirms all throughout scripture. He wants us to share in one another's troubles and problems. And being mindful of healthy self-care means we know the times when others need to be brought into a situation. We're able to admit when we need them to come alongside us in support. And thinking we don't need help or being unwilling to give it is sinful.

It's okay not to be okay. But it's not okay to sit there helpless, especially when we have people who want to help. Be brave and admit you need support, and watch how that support will nourish your soul and ignite joy again.

Dear God, give me the courage and confidence to ask for help and give it when needed. Amen.

A LIVING AND HOLY SACRIFICE

Brothers and sisters, in light of all I have shared with you about God's mercies, I urge you to offer your bodies as a living and holy sacrifice to God, a sacred offering that brings Him pleasure; this is your reasonable, essential worship.

ROMANS 12:1 VOICE

Before we give ourselves away in mercy to those around us, we must give ourselves away in worship to God. Worship reminds us of our position in relationship to the Father, and it keeps us surrendered. But worship doesn't only mean raising our hands as we sing in church. We have the privilege of worshipping with our bodies. It keeps our focus on faith, weighing decisions by asking how it benefits us and blesses the Lord. It's deep intentionality.

If we are to offer our bodies as living and holy sacrifices to God, then it makes sense to do all we can to care for them. We can choose to eat well and get good sleep. We can proactively press the PAUSE button when life feels too big and rest in the Lord. We can saturate ourselves in the Word, nourishing our parched souls. We can unpack our feelings with God. And while He values a servant's heart, if we don't find ways to care for our bodies, we won't have the faith or the energy to worship God through loving others.

Dear God, help me care for my body so I can worship You with it. Amen.

REAPING AND SOWING

Don't be misled; remember that you can't ignore God and get away with it: a man will always reap just the kind of crop he sows! If he sows to please his own wrong desires, he will be planting seeds of evil and he will surely reap a harvest of spiritual decay and death; but if he plants the good things of the Spirit, he will reap the everlasting life that the Holy Spirit gives him.

GALATIANS 6:7–8 TLB

The concept of reaping and sowing is vital for believers to understand and is especially important when it comes to caring for yourself. When you invest time in feeding on God's Word, your soul will be invigorated by scripture so you're able to tackle whatever is ahead. When you're diligent to protect your schedule, ensuring there's space for rest, you will be energized to shine your light in the world. As you work through your difficult feelings with God, weight will be lifted off your shoulders as He restores. And when you choose to be kind to yourself and reject that harsh inner voice, you'll watch joy spill forth from you again.

Dear God, help me to be intentional to sow the right things into my life so I reap the beautiful blessings that will come from You. Help me plant the good things of the Spirit with great expectation. Amen.

COMPARISON IS A THIEF

Let everyone be sure that he is doing his very best, for then he will have the personal satisfaction of work well done and won't need to compare himself with someone else. Each of us must bear some faults and burdens of his own. For none of us is perfect!

GALATIANS 6:4–5 TLB

Comparison is a thief who will steal every bit of joy you have. In sneaky ways, it makes you look at someone else's very best and size it up against your very worst. It keeps you from being content with what you have. And it tells you—in hurtful ways—that you're not good enough. Friend, be done with this pattern of living. Choose to care for yourself by accepting how God made you.

Are you perfect? No. Are you without struggles and challenges? Nope. Is life going to come easily? Probably not. But when you strive to be the best version of yourself, steeped in God's Word and embracing a life of faith, you will find personal satisfaction in pursuing a righteous life. And you won't feel the need to compare yourself for validation because you'll already have it from God.

Dear God, help me do my very best in life without comparing myself along the way. Let me embrace my imperfections as I also embrace Your love. Amen.

DON'T LET THE WORLD MOLD YOU

Do not allow this world to mold you in its own image. Instead, be transformed from the inside out by renewing your mind. As a result, you will be able to discern what God wills and whatever God finds good, pleasing, and complete.

ROMANS 12:2 VOICE

Your mind has a lot of power over the ways you choose to live. It's persuasive, often without you recognizing the connection between what you think and how you act. Your thoughts—your heart—need God's consistent renewal to stay focused on what is good and true and worthy. When we ignore our need for His intervention, the world's ways begin to creep in. We start to believe their narrative. We adopt their coping mechanisms and ideals. And eventually we are left emotionally bankrupt.

God's Word is clear when it says not to allow the world to mold us. It will shape us in all the wrong ways, depleting our souls of hope and joy. It will push us to do more and be more. It will confuse our true feelings, leaving us unable to experience sustainable peace. Rather than rest in truth, our spirits will be unsettled and troubled. And we'll lack the ability to hear God's voice and follow His ways. Care for yourself by always loving Him the most.

Dear God, let the things of this world grow dim as You burn brighter in my life. Amen.

NOT MORE IMPORTANT

Because of the grace allotted to me, I can respectfully tell you not to think of yourselves as being more important than you are; devote your minds to sound judgment since God has assigned to each of us a measure of faith.

ROMANS 12:3 VOICE

Sometimes we take the idea of self-care too far. We may decide it gives us permission to be self-focused above all else. We may think it signals unwavering approval to be selfish. And while God is clear about wanting us to take care of our minds, bodies, and spirits, it doesn't mean we're to consider ourselves more important. We're not better than anyone else because we all have our own races to run. Amen?

Instead, ask God to give you sound judgment so you'll know the parameters of being kind to yourself and loving others. Let Him deepen your faith at the right times so you're able to follow His leading. And focus on staying in your own lane, encouraging your soul, and resting in the Lord so you can shine His glory into the world.

Dear God, I confess the times I've thought of myself as more important than I am. Help me understand Your deep and devoted love for everyone and to act in ways that reflect that truth. Amen.

THE ANTIDOTE TO DISCOURAGEMENT

And let us not get tired of doing what is right, for after a while we will reap a harvest of blessing if we don't get discouraged and give up. That's why whenever we can we should always be kind to everyone, and especially to our Christian brothers.

GALATIANS 6:9–10 TLB

When we commit to self-care, it means doing what we can to put our best foot forward. It may require us to pay more attention to our diets so we're feeding our bodies better. We may need to press the PAUSE button or slow down so our weary soul can rest. It may require us to protect our schedule with ferocity so we have more time for what matters most. We may need to sit with a counselor to unpack the barrage of emotions we're feeling. Regardless, it's important that we take care of ourselves so we have the desire and energy to continue doing what is right. If we don't, it's a setup for discouragement, which often leads us to giving up.

An added blessing brought by this kind of intentional self-care is that it sets us up to encourage others. When we're happy and healthy, our happiness flows effortlessly out toward those we love the most.

Dear God, help me stay vigilant so I don't grow weary as I purpose to do what is right. Remind me to care for myself so I can care for those around me. Amen.

PIECES OF THE PUZZLE

If service is your gift, then serve well. If teaching is your gift, then teach well. If you have been given a voice of encouragement, then use it often. If giving is your gift, then be generous. If leading, then be eager to get started. If sharing God's mercy, then be cheerful in sharing it.

ROMANS 12:7–8 VOICE

Today's verse reminds us of the vital role we play in the church body. Everyone has a gift—a piece—they add to the puzzle to make it complete. Some have the ability to serve others with a beautiful purpose. Some may be teachers, always ready to give helpful or necessary instruction. Others can speak encouragement at levels that deeply move the hearts of people. And still others are talented leaders, cheerful givers, and good news sharers. But if we don't nurture our relationship with the Lord, we'll feel depleted and unable to bring forth our gifts.

The time you spend in God's Word and in His presence directly benefits your spiritual energy. It's how you refuel your spiritual tank. When nothing goes in, little comes out. But when you nourish your soul and nurture your spirit, you'll bring forth your gifts with passion.

Dear God, remind me to stay intimately connected with You as my source so the gifts You've given me can flow unhindered. Amen.

HE KNOWS YOUR NEEDS

"So don't worry at all about having enough food and clothing. Why be like the heathen? For they take pride in all these things and are deeply concerned about them. But your heavenly Father already knows perfectly well that you need them, and he will give them to you if you give him first place in your life and live as he wants you to."

MATTHEW 6:31–33 TLB

Do you realize God already knows your needs? He sees every time you struggle to pay a bill. He sees the empty fridge, even though you're frugal. The Lord understands when your joy and peace are lacking because of difficult circumstances. He knows the times you're depleted by the busyness of life. And scripture says that when you live in righteous ways—ways that please God—He will meet those needs every time. Be it physical needs or emotional ones, God will provide as you make Him a priority.

So be mindful to take care of yourself spiritually. Spend time in the Word. Talk to God throughout the day, sharing the ups and downs you're facing. Surround yourself with godly community that feeds the soul. And let the Lord figure out the rest.

Dear God, what a relief to know You see every need even before I do. And You already know how and when You'll provide. Thank You for caring for me as I live to glorify You. Amen.

A DEEP WELL

Love others well, and don't hide behind a mask; love authentically. Despise evil; pursue what is good as if your life depends on it.
ROMANS 12:9 VOICE

When you are diligent to care for yourself, you have what it takes to care for others. You have a deep well of love and compassion to pull from because you've protected your schedule, nourished your soul, pressed PAUSE, and prioritized rest. Every decision you make toward self-care doesn't have to be selfish. It's not about focusing on yourself for egotistical reasons. And it doesn't have to be greedy. Our choices to support a healthy *us* bring great benefits to those we care about. They allow us to love others well and with pure motives because our hearts are full. We're able to better discern good from evil and right from wrong because our intentionality has cleared our minds. And since we're walking a daily path that follows God's plan, we're able to be authentic in relationships and treat others with kindness and generosity.

Dear God, sometimes I think it's selfish to focus on myself so much. I feel guilty for guarding my heart and protecting my time. But I also know I love best from a full cup. Help me understand how to walk in courage so I can love with confidence. Amen.

TOMORROWS

"So don't be anxious about tomorrow. God will take care of your tomorrow too. Live one day at a time."
MATTHEW 6:34 TLB

Today's verse is essential for women. Why? Because we are notorious for jumping ahead as we plan for what comes next. For many, it's difficult to stay in today, even if for really good reasons. Maybe you're plotting out a work schedule or trying to organize your week for maximum flow. Maybe your kids need you to keep track of projects, playdates, and programs. Maybe your husband travels for his job, leaving you to manage the family calendar around him. Strategizing and outlining the coming days sometimes sparks anxiety. It feels overwhelming to know what's ahead. And you're left stressed about tomorrows.

Friend, when scripture tells us to live one day at a time, it's because the Lord knows our tendencies. There's nothing wrong with mapping out your week, but do so with a faithful heart. Trust that God will give you wisdom and energy to make it work or that He will tweak your schedule for you. Then take a deep breath and let the Lord recharge and restore you so you're ready to tackle the day.

Dear God, thinking about tomorrow often wears me out today. I start stressing, worried about it all. Help me plan with full confidence that You're already working out the details. Amen.

FAITH-BASED SELF-CARE

As for me, God forbid that I should boast about anything except the cross of our Lord Jesus Christ. Because of that cross, my interest in all the attractive things of the world was killed long ago, and the world's interest in me is also long dead.

GALATIANS 6:14 TLB

Caring for ourselves spiritually is vital because it's from there we live our best lives. That deep connection to God helps us see situations clearly. It allows us to prioritize what matters the most and respond accordingly. It gives us a unique perspective to look at our circumstances through the lens of faith. And it keeps us humble, understanding that all good things come from the Lord—not from our hard work or the world's offerings.

So how can you practice faith-based self-care? Make time every day to open the Bible and meditate on scripture. Start a prayer as you wake up, and keep dialoguing with God until you drift off to sleep. Be listening for His responses throughout the day. And invest your time and treasure in things eternal, not earthly.

Dear God, sometimes I forget the need to care for myself spiritually. Rather than make it a priority, I let it slide. But I understand the value it brings me to surrender to You in thanksgiving because it helps the world lose its appeal in my heart. Let it be. Amen.

BEATING OURSELVES UP

Any temptation you face will be nothing new. But God is faithful, and He will not let you be tempted beyond what you can handle. But He always provides a way of escape so that you will be able to endure and keep moving forward.

1 CORINTHIANS 10:13 VOICE

Sometimes we beat ourselves up when we mess up. Rather than extend grace for being imperfect, we respond with harshness and hatred. We decide we're weak and wimpy instead of being kind to ourselves. We feel like a disappointment. And because we think this way, we assume God does too. But that's just not true.

The Lord knows we will face temptation. He is omniscient, meaning God literally knows everything past, present, and future. He is never caught off guard. And in His faithfulness, He caps the level of tempting we will face. It will never be more than we can handle. Even more, when we ask His help to escape the lure, God will give it. Love yourself enough to cry out to the Lord and trust that He will show up.

Dear God, help me to be kind to myself when I face temptations. Remind me that You are here and willing to equip me to stand strong. Strengthen me to resist giving in and feeling shame. You are why I can endure and escape all that tries to entice me. Amen.

WHATEVER YOU DO

So then, whether you eat or drink or whatever you do,
do all to the glory of [our great] God.
1 CORINTHIANS 10:31 AMP

One way to make sure your desire for self-care doesn't become overly self-centered is to focus on glorifying God with each choice. Let this new direction be because you want to find your divine joy again. Let each step forward help you become healthy so you can shine your light in the world. Let the goal of self-care be to nourish your soul and reconnect with God in fresh ways. Let it clear your negative thoughts so you can understand the core of your feelings. And know that when you choose to be kind to yourself, you're choosing to embrace the gift of life.

So, friend, as you journey to health and happiness, invite God into each step. Pray as you make decisions, and listen as He guides you. And no matter what you do, whatever path you are traversing, do it all to the glory of our great God.

Dear God, help my heart to be focused on You with each "me" decision. Help me see the bigger picture with each step I take toward caring for myself so You are glorified in it. I don't want any hint of egotism in my motives. Amen.

LOVING GOD WHOLEHEARTEDLY

Jesus replied, "The most important one is Israel, listen! Our God is the one Lord, and you must love the Lord your God with all your heart, with all your being, with all your mind, and with all your strength."

MARK 12:29–30 CEB

How would walking out today's scripture passage change you? Sometimes we become so self-absorbed with our lives, fixated on getting our needs met, that we become the center of our worlds. Maybe without even realizing it, we set ourselves higher than God because we end up single-minded on what we crave. Verses like the ones above help to ground us in powerful ways, reminding us of what our focus should be.

Rather than be divided, be mindful and aware to love God with all of your heart. Love Him with every fiber of your being, even if imperfectly. Let your thoughts rest on His goodness and the ways He intersects with you on a daily basis. And with your strength, choose to serve Him with every choice and decision. In the end, this is the best self-care plan ever made.

Dear God, help me love You wholeheartedly with all that I am. Let my mind stay fixated on Your goodness over my neediness because I trust You will always provide. Amen.

PUTTING OTHERS FIRST

Live in true devotion to one another, loving each other as sisters and brothers. Be first to honor others by putting them first.

ROMANS 12:10 VOICE

How can we honor others first if we're striving to be good to ourselves? Doesn't self-care override being others-focused? Well, not necessarily. The reality is that when we take steps to make better choices in our lives, we heal. We are restored from brokenness. And that allows us to better show love and compassion toward those around us. So, each decision made to be kind to ourselves pays it forward, if you will.

God's desire is that we have servants' hearts. He tells us the second greatest commandment is to "love your neighbor as yourself" (Mark 12:31 CEB). Being dedicated and loyal to one another is important in God's eyes. But how can we show great concern and compassion when we're gassed by life and running on empty? Let God help you care for yourself so you can care for others.

Dear God, heal and restore me so I can be a blessing to those around me. Help me find perfect ways to honor them by caring for their needs. And fill my heart with compassion so I can be Your hands and feet. Amen.

LOVING HIM ENABLES US TO LOVE OTHERS

"The second [greatest commandment] is this, You will love your neighbor as yourself. No other commandment is greater than these."

MARK 12:31 CEB

This second command comes right after God's first command to love Him wholeheartedly. And if you think about it, it must happen in this order. Because when we choose to love the Lord with all that we are, we are then enabled to love His children with passion and purpose. We are set up to embrace the call to show kindness, compassion, and generosity to others.

When our hearts are turned toward God, He pours out His goodness in abundance. He honors our efforts to do as He has asked. That means that when we follow His lead and press PAUSE or embrace seasons of rest, He will bless it. When we protect our schedule so there's ample time for what matters most, God will bless it. When we dig deeper with Him so our souls are fed from God, our source, He will bless it. And it's from this deep well of blessing that we find the ability and willingness to bless others.

Dear God, fill my heart to its fullest with love for You and the community You've placed in my life. Open my eyes to see the ways You're leading me to be a blessing to others. And heal me from the inside out so I'm able to obey Your commands.

PERMITTED BUT NOT ALWAYS BENEFICIAL

There's a slogan often quoted on matters like this: "All things are permitted." Yes, but not all things are beneficial.

1 CORINTHIANS 10:23 VOICE

What a powerful reminder for believers! God gave each of us free will so we'd be able to make decisions for ourselves. We have the freedom to choose right from wrong, good from evil. But while scripture is clear that all things are permitted, it distinctly mentions that not all things are beneficial.

So, as you're looking for self-care options, invite God into the decision-making process. Does He want you to rearrange your calendar to free up time for different things? Is the Lord asking you to rest in Him rather than trying to fix everything in your own strength? Maybe God is wooing you to spend more time in His presence to bring peace and comfort to your weary soul. Or maybe He's opening doors to new opportunities that will help restore your joy. Regardless, choose to let God lead.

Dear God, thank You for giving me free will. I'm grateful for the gift of choice! But I'm also thankful that You've given guardrails to keep me safe. Help me hear Your voice as I move forward each day. Amen.

ALL BOILS DOWN TO LOVE

"And to love God with all of the heart, a full understanding, and all of one's strength, and to love one's neighbor as oneself is much more important than all kinds of entirely burned offerings and sacrifices."

MARK 12:33 CEB

It all boils down to love, doesn't it? God talks about it constantly in His Word because it's of the utmost importance to His plan for the world. He gives it lavishly and expects it of His children. Scripture even says others will know we are believers by the way we show love. But unless we are emotionally and spiritually healthy, showing love will be challenging.

Ask God to remove anything that hinders your ability to show compassion to those around you. Ask Him to heal the broken places in your heart that received conditional or manipulative love in the past. Let Him help you better understand your muscle memory responses and how love relates to the feelings you're experiencing. Then watch how that flood of God's love enables you to turn around and love others with fervor.

Dear God, sometimes I feel unable to love the way I want to. Maybe it's because of past interactions and relationships. Won't You heal me so I can follow Your commands with passion? Won't You restore me to emotional and spiritual health? I want to be known for my love. Amen.

WORKING TOGETHER

But God has put the body together, giving greater honor to the part with less honor so that there won't be division in the body and so the parts might have mutual concern for each other. If one part suffers, all the parts suffer with it; if one part gets the glory, all the parts celebrate with it. You are the body of Christ and parts of each other.

1 CORINTHIANS 12:24–27 CEB

Just as God fitted the parts of our bodies together to work in unison and agreement, the church is to act in the same manner. We're to act as one, seamlessly. Scripture says we should be so in tune within this community that we should stand together in solidarity. If someone is struggling, we're to join in, providing understanding and support. If there is a reason to celebrate, that too is something we do as a community. But we each have a responsibility in this.

Unless we are intentional to take care of ourselves, what will we be able to bring to the table? If we're worn out by challenging circumstances, how will we have the gumption to stand as a collective? How will we work in sync if bogged down and overwhelmed? Friend, it's vital to take care of yourself God's way. Ask Him to show you.

Dear God, what a privilege and burden to work as a community of believers. Show me how to ensure I'm healthy and ready to support others as we work together for Your kingdom. Amen.

LET YOUR SPIRIT BE ON FIRE

Do not slack in your faithfulness and hard work. Let your spirit be on fire, bubbling up and boiling over, as you serve the Lord.

ROMANS 12:11 VOICE

It's almost impossible for our spirits to be on fire when we are flaming out in life. Marital struggles may be weighing us down, or we may feel underwater as we parent teenagers. A difficult work environment or challenges in finding a job that meets our needs may be causing stress. Maybe we're mourning the loss of a loved one or having trouble finding ways to get through the grieving process itself. Or perhaps overwhelming feelings of dread, insecurity, or fear have us paralyzed and ineffective. So, what do we do?

God wants us to care for ourselves by reaching out to Him for help in these difficulties. He wants us to ask for what we need with courage and confidence. God is ready to intervene at our pleading. Friend, sometimes the only way we can pursue self-care is to humble ourselves and ask for God-care. Don't let anything block or dim your light, especially knowing that God can and will reignite your spark without fail. He will keep you aflame and ready to follow His will and ways. Just ask.

Dear God, keep me burning bright for You in all that I do. Keep me energized and focused on faithfully working to further Your kingdom on earth. I'm all in, Father! Amen.

TRUSTING GOD INSTEAD

Trust God from the bottom of your heart; don't try to figure out everything on your own. Listen for God's voice in everything you do, everywhere you go; he's the one who will keep you on track.

PROVERBS 3:5–6 MSG

Trouble starts brewing when we do the opposite of what today's scripture passage suggests. When we decide we're in charge and able to manage the ups and downs of life without God's guidance, we start to fall apart. Thinking and acting based on our own strength and wisdom sets us up to fail. And often we find ourselves at rock bottom and overwhelmed because we've tried to figure everything out on our own for so long. For this reason, let's change things up.

Friend, we are limited by our humanity. But God experiences no limits. He sees all, knows all, and has every answer we need. And each time we invite Him into our circumstances, the Lord promises to keep us on track. It's His depth of understanding that allows us to stay in alignment with His will for our lives. And it's the best self-care practice we can possess.

Dear God, I confess the times I've moved forward in my own strength without even asking Your opinion. Remind me to look to You for direction and listen for Your voice to lead. Amen.

RUNNING FROM EVIL

Don't assume that you know it all. Run to God! Run from evil! Your body will glow with health, your very bones will vibrate with life!

Proverbs 3:7–8 msg

A key decision that will help your body glow with health is choosing to turn away from sinful, wicked, and immoral things when they come your way. Scripture says that every time you choose good over evil, your "bones will vibrate with life!" If you're wanting to be kind to yourself, make God your first stop when circumstances become challenging. Let Him guide your next steps as you navigate those tricky moments.

Good self-care means being aware of obstacles that might trip you up. Even if something isn't bad in and of itself, it may be bad timing. It may be too much of a good thing. It might eventually lead you down the wrong path. Or it might be corrupt from the start. But in those times, cling to God and let Him steer you clear of harm's way so you can thrive!

Dear God, give me the courage and confidence to choose the things that will bless and not harm me. Help me use godly discernment as I make hard decisions that could easily trip me up. And let me stay close to You when life feels confusing. Amen.

FAITH FIRST

Honor the Lord with your wealth and with the first fruits of all your crops (income); then your barns will be abundantly filled and your vats will overflow with new wine.

Proverbs 3:9–10 AMP

Simply put, give everything to God, especially your firstfruits. And while these verses especially address honoring Him with your finances, this same concept can be applied to why you pursue self-care.

While the Lord doesn't expect you to be cleaned up and perfect, He does want you to invest in a relationship with Him. You can come as you are, sinful and wretched, and He will embrace you with everlasting love. And in those moments—moments we may think are messy—God delights in you coming to Him first. You've honored Him with authentic surrender. And you're trusting He will abundantly fill your heart with hope as He restores and heals. You are believing your Father will bless your choice to have faith—first.

Dear God, I admit it's often hard to come to You first. When life gets tough, my initial desire is to call my friends and family. Maybe I hide away and cry. But I understand the value of going to You first. Help me walk that out in the moment, especially when muscle memory kicks in. I trust You. Amen.

HELPING OTHERS CARE FOR THEMSELVES TOO

We should stop looking out for our own interests and instead focus on the people living and breathing around us.

1 CORINTHIANS 10:24 VOICE

One wonderful way we can focus on others and their well-being is by setting an example with how we care for ourselves. Make no mistake: Your life preaches. If you say one thing but do something different, it speaks loudly. And while taking care of yourself emotionally, physically, and spiritually is very important, encouraging the same in others matters too. Keep that in mind as you do the things that nourish you, body and soul.

When you're careful to protect your schedule, it helps others see how they can do it as well. Being mindful of pressing the PAUSE button at the right moments teaches them to do the same. Each time we choose to unpack our feelings rather than stuff them, those around us see it modeled and are inspired to follow. Essentially, our self-care becomes an example for their self-care.

Dear God, I love the thought that taking care of myself can positively inspire the same in others. Let me be a light that shines into a dark world, helping to bless those around me. And let my pursuit of a healthy heart and mind help others focus on theirs. Amen.

GOD WILL COURSE CORRECT

But don't, dear friend, resent God's discipline; don't sulk under his loving correction. It's the child he loves that God corrects; a father's delight is behind all this.

PROVERBS 3:11–12 MSG

Sometimes God must course correct our lives so we don't go too far in the wrong direction. He may close a door of opportunity when we are in desperate need for rest. He may put up roadblocks if we're dabbling in something that will steal our joy. God may press PAUSE on our behalf if we need to slow down and catch our breath. He may even highlight guilt and shame in an effort to make us be kinder to ourselves.

Rather than be in a huff about it, embrace it. Let it make your heart tender toward your loving Father. In the seasons when you aren't very mindful of self-care, He loves you enough to intervene. Your well-being matters to Him. And God will often make the changes necessary to change the direction you're walking. Listen and watch for the Lord's leading, and thank Him for His compassion.

Dear God, what a relief to know You will step in and correct my course when necessary. And while it may frustrate me at the time, I'm thankful You love me so deeply. Amen.

BEING FULL OF LOVE FOR OTHERS

Be full of love for others, following the example of Christ who loved you and gave himself to God as a sacrifice to take away your sins. And God was pleased, for Christ's love for you was like sweet perfume to him.

EPHESIANS 5:2 TLB

The only way we can be full of love for others is to be filled with God's love first. We can't embrace a servant's heart unless God brings divine perspective, helping us take the focus off what we need and want. We won't be tender and compassionate until we recognize that the Lord is tender and compassionate toward us. Until we follow His lead, letting Him show us how to care for ourselves His way, we'll be unable to serve others with passion and purpose.

What is God asking you to change up in your life? Where is the Holy Spirit nudging you to take a step back and breathe? How is He encouraging you to follow a different path to be healthier emotionally, physically, and spiritually? Be sensitive to God's voice, friend. Listen and watch. Because when you do, His love and care will heal your neglected places so you can love and care for those who matter the most to you.

Dear God, I want to be full of love for others, and I know it starts with You. Heal me and guide me. Amen.

CREATED, KNITTED TOGETHER, AND SET APART

You are the one who created my innermost parts; you knit me together while I was still in my mother's womb. I give thanks to you that I was marvelously set apart. Your works are wonderful—I know that very well.

PSALM 139:13–14 CEB

In today's world, it's easy to struggle with insecurities constantly whispering that we're not good enough. We may struggle with jealousy, always comparing our very worst to others' very best. We may battle with fear that no matter what we do, we will never measure up to the unattainable standards of the world. And because of this, we work overtime to try and make ourselves acceptable. We take self-care to an unhealthy level, tangled with all the wrong motives. In our desperation to be loved by those around us, we forget that in God's eyes, we already are.

From your very beginning, God has been with you. He created you. He knit you together. The Lord set you apart from everyone else on purpose. And you are wonderfully made with great intentionality. Ask God to help you rest in that beautiful truth today.

Dear God, I confess that I sometimes struggle to feel special in this world. Remind me that I am set apart by You, and let that trump my need for earthly adoration. Amen.

THE CURE FOR RECKLESS WORDS

Let there be no sex sin, impurity or greed among you. Let no one be able to accuse you of any such things. Dirty stories, foul talk, and coarse jokes—these are not for you. Instead, remind each other of God's goodness, and be thankful.

EPHESIANS 5:3–4 TLB

The idea behind good and healthy self-care is to better yourself. It can help you replace the energy-draining people and circumstances with joy that comes from the Lord. It can help remove the issues causing your divine light to dim rather than shine brightly. When you're mindful to care for yourself God's way, you'll watch a weary soul be nourished back to full strength. You will have better discernment for when it's time to press the PAUSE button and take a breather. The Lord will help you understand complex feelings so you can be kinder to yourself. With His help, you will be restored to wholeness.

Why is this important? Because when we're living God's way, we won't give in to impurities with ease. We'll have a clear mind to steer away from foul talk. And instead of reckless words, we will have the energy and wherewithal to speak of God's goodness.

Dear God, I want my words to be used to bless others and glorify You. Help me care for myself in ways that make this kind of living a reality. Amen.

A REMINDER TO REJOICE

Do not forget to rejoice, for hope is always just around the corner. Hold up through the hard times that are coming, and devote yourselves to prayer. Share what you have with the saints, so they lack nothing; take every opportunity to open your life and home to others.

ROMANS 12:12–13 VOICE

Today's scripture passage reminds us to rejoice in those times when we're feeling depleted by life. When hopelessness sets up camp in our hearts, the best thing we can do for ourselves is worship the Lord for who He is. We can praise Him for what He has done in our lives before and what He will do next. In tough moments, we can go to God in prayer and pour out from the depths of our hearts with authenticity and freedom. And we can encourage one another to position ourselves in a faith posture, always pointing back to the Lord's goodness. These intentional choices set our expectations on what is right and who is true.

Even more, doing this allows you to stay emotionally and spiritually healthy no matter what comes your way. Anytime you fix your eyes on Jesus, comfort, hope, and peace follow.

Dear God, sometimes it's hard for me to rejoice when I feel hopeless. Help me remember that You are ready and willing to bring healing and restoration to my heart every time. Amen.

YOUR ANXIETY

Examine me, God! Look at my heart! Put me to the test! Know my anxious thoughts! Look to see if there is any idolatrous way in me, then lead me on the eternal path!

PSALM 139:23–24 CEB

With a bold request, the psalmist showed great faith in God's ability to bring comfort and calm to quiet his anxiousness. He knew without any doubt that God was the only one who could shift his current direction onto the path leading to Him. But recognize the part the psalmist had to play in this scenario.

While he understood God to be the healer, the writer still had to cry out for healing. He had to lay himself bare before God, surrendered to the process of deep examination and heart work. He had to be willing for God to remove and restore, even knowing it might be a painful process. He fully trusted God to work in his life so that necessary change could happen. His self-care routine was an intentional choice to surrender to the one who could fix and heal. Let's follow his lead.

Dear God, thank You for being a safe place to share my deepest worries. I can be honest and real with You, and I love it. And rather than judge me, thank You for restoring my mind and heart to healthy places. Amen.

GOD IS WITH YOU ALWAYS

The Eternal One will never leave you; He will lead you in the way that you should go. When you feel dried up and worthless, God will nourish you and give you strength. And you will grow like a garden lovingly tended; you will be like a spring whose water never runs out.

ISAIAH 58:11 VOICE

God is the one who will care for your every need. He will provide at every turn. And today's scripture affirms this truth, reminding us that we're never without His holy presence. So be comforted knowing God's promise never to leave you alone is unbreakable. Even when you feel abandoned, the simple truth is you are not. When you feel worthless and depleted, His presence will bring much-needed nourishment. He will strengthen you to stand strong. And as you pray for guidance and deliverance, the Lord will reveal the path you can follow to find comfort as you realign your heart to His.

Did you notice what God's intervention will bring forth from you? Isaiah said we'll experience personal and spiritual growth, as well as the ability to maintain a settled spirit as we pour out to others. And it will be in abundance.

Dear God, Your presence is the most precious thing to me. Let me feel it every day as it leads me toward a healthier way to live out each day. Amen.

MEADOWS AND STREAMS

Because the Lord is my Shepherd, I have everything I need! He lets me rest in the meadow grass and leads me beside the quiet streams. He gives me new strength. He helps me do what honors him the most.

PSALM 23:1–3 TLB

When life feels harried and hurried, the thought of resting in meadow grass enables us to exhale. Can't you imagine a gentle breeze washing over you while you take in nature? Without any worry, you lie there and soak in the sun. Maybe the idea of quiet streams is more to your liking. Getting to prop yourself up on a tree trunk while listening to the water gently trickle by is the relaxation you're looking for. This is where your soul comes alive as the stress washes away. Regardless of which scenario connects most, understand that calm is available to you as you rest in the Lord. And it's through this rest that your strength is restored.

Putting yourself in the arms of God is the best self-care decision you can make, because time with the Lord is time well invested, and it will empower you to make good choices that benefit you and glorify Him.

Dear God, thank You for painting a picture of rest for me. I want to be with You to rest and recharge. Help me trust You when I'm feeling overwhelmed and struggling to catch my breath. Amen.

THIS LITTLE LIGHT OF MINE

For though once your heart was full of darkness, now it is full of light from the Lord, and your behavior should show it! Because of this light within you, you should do only what is good and right and true.

Ephesians 5:8–9 TLB

As believers, we have a beautiful light that shines God's goodness into the world. Once we accepted Jesus as our personal Savior—recognizing Him as God's only Son who died on the cross for our sins and rose three days later—the Holy Spirit took up permanent residence in our hearts. He is the light within that radiates out for others to see. That light is a noticeable compassion and kindness that draws attention. It's acts of goodness where there are few. And it's designed to point others to the Father in heaven.

When we don't do the necessary things to feed our souls and ignite our spirits, this light dims. Being worn out by life shuts us down. And when we're unable to rest in the Lord because our calendars are packed, the light flickers. Let God show you how to keep your light shining.

Dear God, help me keep the light within bright and shining. You rescued me from the darkness, and I want my life to be like a lighthouse, always pointing others to You. Amen.

SPIRITUALLY HEALTHY FROM THE INSIDE OUT

If someone mistreats you because you are a Christian, don't curse him; pray that God will bless him.
ROMANS 12:14 TLB

Sometimes we read a passage of scripture that feels too hard to walk out. It seems impossible because it's counter to what our human nature wants us to do. And we worry because it looks as if we're set up to fail. Unless we are in good spiritual health, these hard verses will be super challenging indeed. So how can we maintain a healthy faith?

It may vary from person to person, but what is universal is choosing to stay connected to the heart of God. That takes intentional time in His presence, opening the Word daily to see what He says about living. It's spending time in prayer, recognizing His goodness, unpacking the heaviness we feel, and listening for His answers. It's making the hard choices to obey the commands He has set forth, understanding that blessings flow from them. And it's being healthy enough emotionally to show love and compassion to those who hurt us first. Friend, we can only do that with God healing us from the inside out.

Dear God, help me put in the time to grow my faith so I can obey with a pure heart. Help me lean on You for strength to make it so. Amen.

THE DARK VALLEY

Even when walking through the dark valley of death I will not be afraid, for you are close beside me, guarding, guiding all the way.

PSALM 23:4 TLB

The reality is that we will all walk through the dark valley more than once in our lifetime. The Bible is clear that in our time here on planet Earth, we will have troubles. It's not a matter of *if* we will; it's a matter of *when*. But as we have our faith solidified in Jesus, there is no reason to let fear steal our joy. It doesn't have to extinguish the light we have inside. Instead, God's presence with us is guaranteed, and He will get us through those tough times without fail. And as we choose to rest in Him, our soul will be nourished and able to find hope again.

Friend, there are times God calls us to care for ourselves, and other times we're told to let Him be the caretaker. But regardless, He is with us through every up and down life brings. We can always count on God to guard and guide each step as we trust Him with all our hearts.

Dear God, I will not be afraid of the dark valleys, because I have You to help navigate me through those times. Thank You for never leaving me alone. Amen.

SHINE THE LIGHT OF JESUS INSTEAD

Brothers and sisters, don't waste your breath complaining about one another. If you judge others, you will be judged yourself. Be very careful! You will face the one true Judge who is right outside the door.

JAMES 5:9 VOICE

Choosing to sit in judgment of others sets us up to be judged ourselves. Today's scripture is clearly warning us to steer clear of being critical of those around us because judgment boomerangs. Do you know what else it does? It plants a bitter seed in our spirits that keeps us stirred up and unable to rest. We begin to focus on what others are doing that annoys us rather than focusing on loving them with God's help. We obsess about their shortcomings as something negative instead of coming alongside them in support. And it steals our joy.

What if, instead, you chose to shine the light of Jesus in their direction? What if you invested in prayer about your feelings, asking God to remove your judgmental spirit and fill you with love and compassion? Let Jesus bring nourishment to your soul so you can look at others through a full heart of goodness.

Dear God, forgive me for the times I've sat in judgment of others. I understand that it's not my place and that it also opens me up to judgment in return. Bolster my body and soul to love instead. Amen.

BEING PURSUED ALWAYS

Certainly Your faithful protection and loving provision will pursue me where I go, always, everywhere. I will always be with the Eternal, in Your house forever.
PSALM 23:6 VOICE

What a gift to know God is always pursuing us. In those moments when we feel worthless or unloved, the reality is that it's not true—at least not according to God. We may feel tossed aside by certain friends. Some family members may have written us off. We might struggle to feel included in the office or in the neighborhood. Our calendars may be wide open, and not because we're wanting them to be. But without question, God will always be pursuing us with passion and purpose because His love never fails.

Today, let that fact bring much-needed nourishment to your soul. Let it bring hope to your weary heart. Let the truth that God won't ever leave you, no matter where you go or what you're battling, bring encouragement. And choose to rest in that beautiful blessing, especially when bombarded with feelings of insignificance. You matter greatly to your Creator.

Dear God, it does my heart good to know You will always see value in me. Bring that to mind every time I begin to feel unseen and unimportant. Let it be what bolsters my soul to stand strong when I'm struggling. Amen.

THE BLESSING OF TOGETHERNESS

When others are happy, be happy with them.
If they are sad, share their sorrow.
ROMANS 12:15 TLB

Whether you're down in the dumps or up in the clouds, reach out to your friends. Call on your family. It's important that we surround ourselves with those who can join us in calamity or celebration. We need them to stand with us in the storm or in the sunshine. For our emotional and mental health, we need a community of people to bring help or a hallelujah at the right time. God's plan has always been for us to experience the powerful blessing of togetherness.

Think about it: Who are the ones you consider to be your tribe? Who are the people you can always count on to provide encouragement or excitement when you need it most? Who helps you find joy or find the energy to keep shining your light into the world? Who helps you better understand your feelings? Who loves you without fail? Friend, keep those wonderful people close and choose to love them with the same goodness in return.

Dear God, thank You for the blessing of togetherness. You've given me an amazing group of people to call my family and friends. Help me always to love them well as I feel their love reach out to me. Amen.

WHERE ARE YOU DESPERATE FOR RESTORATION?

Learn as you go along what pleases the Lord. Take no part in the worthless pleasures of evil and darkness.
EPHESIANS 5:10–11 TLB

At times we all indulge in self-care. We might try to eat and sleep better and get more regular exercise. We might spend money on facials or pedicures. We might invest in Christian counseling to find healing from issues that continue to trip us up in life. We might even try to be intentional in finding balance between work and play so we don't burn out. But it's vital we choose carefully so we don't embrace worthless pleasures that lead us away from God's will. Sometimes they are obvious, and other times not so much.

The best self-care is God-care. Invite Him into the places you're feeling desperate for restoration or rejuvenation. Let the Lord guide you along the path of His goodness, for you can trust His leading. God already knows where you are lacking. He sees where you are depleted. And He understands the depth and complexity of all you are feeling. Ask God to care for your heart and mind and soul. Then watch as He does so in fresh ways that bring back hope and joy.

Dear God, show me the ways that please You so I steer clear of indulging in worthless pleasures as I pursue restoration. Amen.

YOU'RE NOT SUPERWOMAN

You spread out a table before me, provisions in the midst of attack from my enemies; You care for all my needs, anointing my head with soothing, fragrant oil, filling my cup again and again with Your grace.

PSALM 23:5 VOICE

Sometimes we go into overdrive, trying to make sure every need we have is met. We take on the burden of being a superwoman. And rather than ask our family and friends for help and bring each burden to God in prayer, we double down and go solo. We move into task mode and heap all sorts of unrealistic expectations on ourselves. And then when we fail—because we aren't superhuman—our inner critic beats us up. We're left in worse emotional and mental condition than before. But God doesn't want this.

Scripture says God is engaged in our lives and promises to care for every need with perfection, even if it looks different than we thought or hoped. He will bring comfort to our weary souls and bring healing to the broken places. And God's abundance will never run dry, for He will fill us over and over with what we need to stand strong, because He's full of grace. You don't need to be a superwoman.

Dear God, I confess the times I've considered myself to be a superwoman, refusing to look to You for help and hope. Thank You for knowing each need and promising to meet it unconditionally. Amen.

THRIVING NOT STRIVING

Work happily together. Don't try to act big. Don't try to get into the good graces of important people, but enjoy the company of ordinary folks. And don't think you know it all!

ROMANS 12:16 TLB

Do you ever find yourself striving to be someone important? Maybe you want to be more popular or more loved. Maybe you want others to pursue your influence or friendship. Are there times you try to work your way into the "it" crowd, thinking that will open more doors of opportunity? Do you see yourself as better than others, often struggling with entitlement? Is it hard for you to work with certain people because you feel superior? These are tough questions, but being honest jump-starts your journey toward emotional health.

God's desire is for us to thrive in community, not strive to be better than those in it. He wants us to find a place with loving and kind people who minister to our hearts in wonderful ways, because He'll use them to bring hope and healing. When we play well with others, we are more joyful. And as we care for those around us, we'll be caring for ourselves at the same time.

Dear God, I confess the times I've striven to be someone different from who You created me to be and it messed with my confidence. Thank You for reminding me that I am fearfully and wonderfully made. Amen.

THE COMMON THREAD OF WORRY

"Look at the birds! They don't worry about what to eat—they don't need to sow or reap or store up food—for your heavenly Father feeds them. And you are far more valuable to him than they are. Will all your worries add a single moment to your life?"

MATTHEW 6:26–27 TLB

As women, we have a common thread that knits us together—worry—because so much pulls our heartstrings. We often feel apprehension for our kids as they navigate hard moments of life. We experience fear in marriage, especially in difficult seasons when we struggle to connect. We agonize over financial constraints and feel uneasy about health issues. When our calendars are packed, we feel the burden of busyness sitting squarely on our shoulders. And rather than leave these burdens at the feet of Jesus, we find ourselves tightly tangled instead.

Let part of your self-care routine be prayer. Start a conversation with God when you awake and weave it throughout the day until you drift off at night. When worries come, pass them off to your loving Father, and watch as He unravels each knot.

Dear God, I admit that worry is a big tangle that challenges me every day. I can't seem to get a handle on it. Help me to be quick to pray when it comes, trusting You to work all things for my good and Your glory. Amen.

THE CONFIDENCE WE NEED

It is even more important, my brothers and sisters, that you remember not to make a vow by the heavens or the earth or by anything. When you say "yes," it should always mean "yes," and "no" should always mean "no." If you can keep your word, you will avoid judgment.

JAMES 5:12 VOICE

Confidence can sometimes be challenging to have and to hold. When we're feeling insecure about ourselves, it's common to shy away from being bold. Not only are we battling thoughts of inadequacy, but we are also struggling to find the courage to say what we really mean. The guts and grit it takes to be honest feel too far away, so we struggle to let our "yes" be "yes" and our "no" be "no."

When you're mindful to be kind to yourself, it helps you feel stronger. Too often we are self-critical and say things that are degrading. We can be our own worst enemies, sometimes not even realizing our negative self-talk. But when we invest in our relationship with God and ask Him to bring healing and restoration, we'll be able to stand in His confidence. God's love will strengthen us in the right ways.

Dear God, I don't like to be wishy-washy with my words. I want to speak with resolve and purpose. Help me to be confident in what I say. Amen.

OPENING UP TO OTHERS

So own up to your sins to one another and pray for one another. In the end, you may be healed. Your prayers are powerful when they are rooted in a righteous life.

JAMES 5:16 VOICE

While it may be one of the most difficult things to do at times, being honest is freeing. To off-load what's burdening you to a trusted friend or family member often feels like a one-hundred-pound weight off your chest. To pray for one another with all secrets on the table is powerful. We're not meant to carry our struggles alone, and sharing them sets us up for healing and restoration.

But realize that the enemy wants you to keep sins hidden because then he can taunt you with them. He can heap shame and guilt on you. But his plans fall flat when you share. And each time you do, it's a self-care decision that brings freedom and healing.

Friend, God designed community to help empower you to walk out a life of faith. But be wise in who you open up to, because not everyone has earned the right to hear your heart. Ask God to show you who will listen and love faithfully.

Dear God, I'm scared to share my struggles because I'm afraid of being judged. Guide me to the people I can trust. And then give me the ability to open up appropriately. Amen.

MAKING ALLOWANCES

Be humble and gentle. Be patient with each other, making allowance for each other's faults because of your love. Try always to be led along together by the Holy Spirit and so be at peace with one another.

EPHESIANS 4:2–3 TLB

It's hard to be at peace with others when we're at war with ourselves. At times the chaos fogs up any chance at harmony. When we show little patience in our own lives, extending patience to those around us feels almost impossible. And as we beat ourselves up for failing once again, we often have the same response when others are imperfect too. We need to be kinder to ourselves, and that's something we can do only with God's perspective and help.

The more we invest in our relationship with the Lord, the more we begin to see *us* through His eyes. We set aside jealousy because we understand we were made on purpose. We forgo comparison since the Word tells us we're a unique creation. Envy begins to melt away as we see the wonderful gifts that God intentionally baked into us at conception. And embracing our differences allows us to embrace their differences too.

Dear God, I know that when I'm hard on myself I'm often also hard on others. Help me embrace who You made me to be so I can make allowances for myself and those around me. Amen.

YOUR LITTLE LIGHT

Never pay back evil for evil. Do things in such a way that everyone can see you are honest clear through.

ROMANS 12:17 TLB

If your goal is to let your little light shine into the world, then it's important to care for your spiritual health. How can you point others to God if you're a hot mess? It's not about having a problem-free life. That's impossible. But what will speak the loudest is how you function in that mess. Will you let life bring you down and live defeated? Will you stew over an issue and talk of ways to get revenge? Will you walk around angry? Or will you activate your faith?

Spiritual health is important because it's what keeps us calm in chaos. It's how we stand through the storms. It's how we love the unlovable and forgive the unforgivable. And every time you invest in your relationship with God through time in the Word, conversations through prayer, and fellowship with other believers, your ability to live a righteous and honest life improves. It's from there that your little light shines the brightest.

Dear God, just as I try to care for myself physically and emotionally, let me also see the value in taking care of my spiritual health. I know that when I invest in my faith, it shines Jesus into the world. Amen.

FURTHERING THE KINGDOM

So be careful how you act; these are difficult days. Don't be fools; be wise: make the most of every opportunity you have for doing good. Don't act thoughtlessly, but try to find out and do whatever the Lord wants you to.

EPHESIANS 5:15–17 TLB

One powerful reason to be intentional in taking care of yourself is because you have a calling on your life. God has planned something specifically for you, and it's a beautiful mission to further His kingdom. If you are feeling overwhelmed because you've neglected yourself, there's a good chance you'll shut down. Too often fatigue renders us ineffective. And, friend, that's just not acceptable because we are here to point others to God.

Are you overtired and unmotivated? Take inventory of your life to see what needs to change. Do you need to take a step back from a commitment? Do you need to better protect your schedule? Do you need to process through feelings? Do you need to spend more time in the Word? Scripture tells us to be wise, act with intention, seize opportunities to do good, and let God lead. To do that, we must make smart choices each day.

Dear God, thank You for creating me with a calling! I want to faithfully walk the path You planned in advance for me, making the most of every opportunity to do good. Amen.

NEW LIFE

Let me say this, then, speaking for the Lord: Live no longer as the unsaved do, for they are blinded and confused. Their closed hearts are full of darkness; they are far away from the life of God because they have shut their minds against him, and they cannot understand his ways.

EPHESIANS 4:17–18 TLB

As believers, we're blessed to have new lives. Where we used to live for ourselves—focused on what we wanted and desired—our eyes are now wide open. Our hearts are no longer closed off from God's goodness. Our minds aren't clouded by darkness. The Holy Spirit who now resides within us helps guide our words and actions to reflect this new and beautiful life. And as we grow in our relationship with God, we crave connection to Him through prayer and His Word so we can better understand His will and ways.

This is how the Lord's light shines from you into the world. Accepting Jesus as your personal Savior, believing He is the Son of God who died on the cross for your sins, changes you. And that change is visible to others. As your life preaches—as your light shines—it opens the door for God to capture others' hearts too. Be mindful to care for your spiritual health because it helps point to the Father in heaven.

Dear God, thank You for a new life that can influence others for You. Amen.

CHOOSING AN OBEDIENT LIFE

Good friend, don't forget all I've taught you; take to heart my commands. They'll help you live a long, long time, a long life lived full and well.

PROVERBS 3:1–2 MSG

Every time you choose to follow God's commands, it's like self-care on steroids. You could work out all day long, eat everything green and organic, sleep a full eight hours every night, and remove stress from your life, and those things still wouldn't beat obedience. When God directs your path through His Word and prayer, it's not a mere suggestion. It's not just a good idea. The Lord isn't tossing out random thoughts. Instead, He is showing you a path forward into His beautiful plans for your life.

You can work all you want to be physically, mentally, and emotionally healthy. And while there is definite value in doing so, nothing trumps being spiritually healthy by choosing an obedient life. Why? Because it opens the door for His blessings to come spilling through. And scripture says it will help you live a long life that will be full and good.

Dear God, I want to take to heart Your commands. I want to be obedient at every turn because I know it will be for my good and Your glory. Help me live a long, full life following Your will and ways. Amen.

OUT WITH THE OLD

Then you know to take off your former way of life, your crumpled old self—that dark blot of a soul corrupted by deceitful desire and lust—to take a fresh breath and to let God renew your attitude and spirit. Then you are ready to put on your new self, modeled after the very likeness of God: truthful, righteous, and holy.

EPHESIANS 4:22–24 VOICE

Today's verse is a powerful reminder that it's because we know Jesus and are committed to growing deeper in our faith that we're to let this supernatural change take place in us. Rather than try to hold on to our old, sinful ways, we're to be on guard so we don't slip backward. Our former way of life only leads to spiritual death, and we want no part of that.

Let's choose instead to walk away from all that threatens to corrupt us. Let's run toward God and embrace His promise to nourish our souls. When we surrender our crumpled old selves, He lovingly and constantly renews our attitudes and spirits daily. And as we put on our new self that reflects God's goodness, we will find wholeness in Him.

Dear God, thank You for daily renewal. I need it desperately. Let my cry be "Out with the old and in with the new!" Amen.

KEEPING BITTERNESS AT BAY

Make a clean break with all cutting, backbiting, profane talk. Be gentle with one another, sensitive. Forgive one another as quickly and thoroughly as God in Christ forgave you.

EPHESIANS 4:31–32 MSG

Every day, people and circumstances we face bring frustration. It could be struggles with coworkers who are dropping the ball. It could be kids acting disrespectful and disobedient. Maybe your husband's travel schedule is nuts, and you're carrying more responsibility than usual. Maybe a friend was insensitive when you needed her the most. Are you dealing with aging parents? Could financial stress be weighing you down? Have you been neglecting self-care and feeling the effects? These are the kinds of things that sharpen our edges. Amen?

However, doing a good job of taking care of yourself will keep bitterness at bay. Sleeping enough, eating well, and exercising regularly are fantastic, but choosing to protect time with the Lord will soften you in positive ways. Rather than reckless words, joy will flow out. Instead of harsh responses, others will see your gentleness. And you'll be more able to keep short accounts and release offenses.

Dear God, many things have the potential to make me angry, but I don't want to be a bitter woman. Help me take care of myself so I'm able to love others well and live in peace. Amen.

NO MORE LIES

What this adds up to, then, is this: no more lies, no more pretense. Tell your neighbor the truth. In Christ's body we're all connected to each other, after all. When you lie to others, you end up lying to yourself.

Ephesians 4:25 msg

The Bible is crystal clear when it comes to lying, and with good reason! Few things can tear apart relationships more than dishonesty. And because God made us to thrive in community, anything that threatens to break our connection with others is dangerous. People are important to our mental health because they traverse the ups and downs with us. When we need support in a crisis, they hold us tight. When we are desperate for boots-on-the-ground help, they show up. In moments when we don't know what we need, they cover all the bases. They are often the joy bringers, the light shiners, the wisdom givers, and the soul fillers we need the very most.

Even if it's difficult, even if you're worried about being judged, even if you're risking their anger, choose to tell the truth. Be a woman of integrity who walks out her faith honestly. Not only is this caring for them, but it's caring enough about yourself to protect those important relationships.

Dear God, keep my lips from lying to those around me. Help me to be full of truth at all times. Amen.

BECAUSE PEACE IS THE GOAL

Don't quarrel with anyone. Be at peace with everyone, just as much as possible.
ROMANS 12:18 TLB

Sometimes when we fight with others we become confused. In our hurt or anger, we may lose sight of the root issue. We struggle to understand the complexity of our emotions because we're too close to the matter. We get lost in the discussion. And rather than see the bigger picture, we major on the minors and stew.

Be ready and willing to take a break from hard conversations if you need to press PAUSE and regroup. If you would benefit from a breather, then advocate for yourself. If you're having a hard time staying engaged, be honest with the other person. And in those moments, ask the Lord for clarity. He's not a God of confusion and will help simplify the situation so you can better understand your feelings. Once you can speak with clarity and hear with intention, you can find resolution that will usher in peace. And peace is the goal because it's what God wants of all believers.

Dear God, I sometimes get confused when I'm quarreling, and I know that is not from You. When I get there, remind me that I can ask for clarity and You will bring it. Help me trust You for revelation so I can get to peace faster. Amen.

CONNECTING ON THE REGULAR

Talk with each other much about the Lord, quoting psalms and hymns and singing sacred songs, making music in your hearts to the Lord. Always give thanks for everything to our God and Father in the name of our Lord Jesus Christ.

EPHESIANS 5:19–20 TLB

When we are emotionally and spiritually healthy, our outlook on life is often positive. Even if going through a tough storm, we have hope because we know God is with us. We are confident things will work out for our good and His glory. It doesn't mean it's easy, and it doesn't mean we're happy about the challenges, but a robust faith allows us to find joy regardless of difficult circumstances. It gives us a fresh perspective that leads to a heart of gratitude. And when we invest time in a Christian community, we're surrounded by those who can encourage us, worship with us, and remind us of God's perfect track record of provision.

Be intentional to connect with the Father regularly because you need His guidance as you try to navigate this crazy world. And make godly community a priority, knowing that other believers will remind you to look up.

Dear God, give me the desire to worship You daily. It's not only good for my emotional and spiritual health, but it also helps me bring hope to those around me. Amen.

CLEAR THINKING AND COMMON SENSE

Dear friend, guard Clear Thinking and Common Sense with your life; don't for a minute lose sight of them. They'll keep your soul alive and well, they'll keep you fit and attractive.

PROVERBS 3:21–22 MSG

As you set healthy goals, let the pursuit of wisdom and common sense top the list. Understanding what is true and right and walking these out in the different areas of your life is a part of your faith journey. These two will keep you safe from stumbling. They will help you steer clear of disaster, debacle, and defeat. And just like everything else that's important, you'll need to guard them because they may easily slip away when life gets busy.

But, friend, you're not alone in this mission to find clear thinking and common sense. This worthy quest is not all up to you. God will offer direction and protection. When you ask for it, He will fortify your resolve so your soul stays nourished and alive. And as you fully embrace wisdom and common sense in your daily walk, you will find a beautiful strength.

Dear God, help me grab on to wisdom and common sense with fervor, setting them as priorities each day. And help me slow down when I need to make decisions, so I can choose wisely through those lenses. Amen.

ONLY JESUS

I have been crucified with Christ [that is, in Him I have shared His crucifixion]; it is no longer I who live, but Christ lives in me. The life I now live in the body I live by faith [by adhering to, relying on, and completely trusting] in the Son of God, who loved me and gave Himself up for me.

GALATIANS 2:20 AMP

For many, Galatians 2:20 is a very confusing verse. It's hard to understand how we've shared in Jesus' death while still alive and breathing air on planet Earth. But this passage in Galatians is a powerful truth that will help us live with joy and peace.

Paul was revealing that because of Jesus, the law no longer applied to him. Being a believer had set him free through Christ's death on the cross, just as if he had been hanging there too. The law has been replaced by faith, which is wonderful news since the law could never make us right with God. Only Jesus can do that. And it's with hearts of gratitude that we're able to live each day in the freedom faith brings. Rest in this today and be filled with joy.

Dear God, thank You for the freedom Jesus has brought to my life. Thank You for freedom from the law I could never follow. Thank You for making a way to be right in Your sight. Amen.

BEING A CHEERFUL GIVER

Giving grows out of the heart—otherwise, you've reluctantly grumbled "yes" because you felt you had to or because you couldn't say "no," but this isn't the way God wants it. For we know that "God loves a cheerful giver."

2 CORINTHIANS 9:7 VOICE

Being a cheerful giver comes from time spent in the Lord's presence. It's understanding—at least as much as we can as humans—the generosity of God. It's realizing the kindness He extends to those who love Him. It's finding peace in our circumstances as we watch God provide in the most meaningful ways. And once we focus our eyes and thoughts on what a gracious Father we have, our heart begins to grow tender toward others. Any reluctant grumbling falls away as we recognize every good thing we have is from God.

So be bighearted and bountiful as you bless those around you. Be it your time or your treasure, look for chances to contribute with gusto. Live with your hands open, palms up, so you don't grab on to anything worldly as security. And let your light shine God's goodness into the world. As you have opportunity, give with joy because you want to honor God through your giving.

Dear God, let me be a giver to reflect the generosity I've seen in You. Make my heart tender and eager to share of myself and my resources. They're Yours anyway. Amen.

REVENGE IS NOT THE WAY

Dear friends, never avenge yourselves. Leave that to God, for he has said that he will repay those who deserve it. Don't take the law into your own hands.
ROMANS 12:19 TLB

You may be diligent to care for yourself, but be sure that doesn't include settling the score with others. Advocating is admirable, but revenge isn't. Scripture is very clear that taking matters into your own hands isn't God's plan. You're not to retaliate or hit back, even when it feels right. Self-care isn't the same as self-defense.

Instead, surrender every hurt to the Lord. Go to Him in prayer each time you're tempted to get even, because God is your protector. He is the one who can restore your broken heart and fill it with deep joy. He will reenergize a weary soul back to health. God will reignite the beautiful light of Jesus you carry inside so it shines brightly again. And when you submit your hurt into His hands rather than strike back at others yourself, He will hold you up. God will repay those who deserve it, allowing you to stay in a righteous state of mind.

Dear God, be quick to intervene when I'm hurting to remind me that revenge is not the right response. I know You are my protector and will take matters into Your capable hands so I can rest and trust. Amen.

IT'S OKAY TO BE ANGRY

Go ahead and be angry. You do well to be angry—but don't use your anger as fuel for revenge. And don't stay angry. Don't go to bed angry. Don't give the Devil that kind of foothold in your life.

EPHESIANS 4:26–27 MSG

There is something liberating about anger. When we take the time to dig deep and understand our feelings, anger is often the only response that can come from it. Life is unfair and hurt is real. And what a gift to know that God understands why we feel incensed at times. Even more, what a blessing to realize that anger isn't a sin, because God is the one who gave us the ability to feel it. There are, however, limits.

Part of being kind to yourself is choosing not to embrace shame or guilt for feeling certain ways. We're complex human beings with a range of emotions. When anger emerges, it's okay as long as we move past it. If we're not plotting revenge, let's feel it. But let's also remember that holding on only opens the door for the enemy to get a foothold and make it fester into unforgiveness.

Dear God, what a gift to know anger isn't sinful if I feel it within certain parameters. Thank You for validating my feelings while encouraging me to be kind to myself at the same time. Amen.

STORING HEAVENLY TREASURES

"Don't store up treasures here on earth where they can erode away or may be stolen. Store them in heaven where they will never lose their value and are safe from thieves. If your profits are in heaven, your heart will be there too."

MATTHEW 6:19–21 TLB

Consider that the self-care you exact here on earth, if done right, will be stored in heaven for you. If you are serious about your spiritual growth and spend consistent time in God's Word, you will be blessed. Every minute you devote to prayer will set your heart on heavenly things. When you praise and worship through music, that sweet connection will allow the Lord to speak deeper into your spirit. Having a servant's heart toward others keeps your eyes on what matters to God. And shining kindness and generosity into a dark and self-centered world helps to further His kingdom in meaningful ways. This is how you store up treasures in heaven.

Don't just care for your body and mind in this life. Care also for your soul, letting it be nourished right from God, your source, so you have His perspective on how to live out the time you've been given here on earth.

Dear God, let everything I store up be with my eyes on eternity, because that is where my heart is focused. Amen.

BLESSINGS IN ABUNDANCE

God can pour on the blessings in astonishing ways so that you're ready for anything and everything, more than just ready to do what needs to be done. As one psalmist puts it, He throws caution to the winds, giving to the needy in reckless abandon. His right-living, right-giving ways never run out, never wear out.

2 CORINTHIANS 9:8–9 MSG

Be encouraged in the truth that God is ready and willing to bless in extraordinary ways. He is able to meet your every need with abundance. And the Lord often gifts those He loves with reckless abandon. He is a good, good Father who lavishes His goodness on believers in a meaningful fashion.

That means when you're wiped out by a hectic schedule or overwhelmed by harrowing emotions, God is fully present with you and ready to restore. When you can't find peace and you crave comfort, He will give you what you need in the moment. God will bless you with fresh joy and nourish your parched soul with passion so you're able to reengage in life with a reinvigorated purpose. And when you're lacking, He will fill you and reestablish your confidence.

Dear God, in a world that is often stingy, thank You for being the God of abundance. I'm blessed by all the ways You're ready and willing to meet my needs. I love You. Amen.

THE SPIRIT OF TRUTH

I will ask the Father to send you another Helper, the Spirit of truth, who will remain constantly with you. The world does not recognize the Spirit of truth, because it does not know the Spirit and is unable to receive Him. But you do know the Spirit because He lives with you, and He will dwell in you.

John 14:16–17 VOICE

If you're a believer—confessing that Jesus is God's only Son who died on the cross as payment for your sins and rose three days later—then you have the Holy Spirit residing within you. As scripture says, He is the Spirit of truth who will never leave you, not for one minute. And when you're in need of help, hope, or healing, He will lead you to the Father.

Sometimes we think it best to try navigating the hard times alone. Maybe it's because we're embarrassed that our lives are messy. Maybe we don't want anyone to know what's happening. Or maybe we are worried that God may be annoyed we find ourselves here again. But His Spirit dwells in us to guide us toward health. God already knows everything on our plate and will bring perfect truth and divine therapy when we need it.

Dear God, what a gift to know Your Spirit resides in me as my personal helper. Thank You for always making a way to feel closer to You. Amen.

WHEN PANIC SETS IN

No need to panic over alarms or surprises, or predictions that doomsday's just around the corner, because God will be right there with you; he'll keep you safe and sound.
PROVERBS 3:25–26 MSG

Panic can negatively affect our bodies. And while this isn't a surprise to learn, many things we may face have the potential to create panic. Think of bad news that arrives unannounced. Unexpected test results from a doctor's visit or an unforeseen increase in a bill can make your heart pound. Discovering inappropriate browsing on the family computer can make your heart sick. Finding evidence of bad choices in your child's bedroom while cleaning or learning about your husband's betrayal out of the blue can put your life in a spin. In those hard moments when panic sets in, remember that God is with you.

Let your heavenly Father usher in peace and comfort when your body is reacting to bad news. Take deep breaths as you rest in His presence. Ask Him to bring perspective as He restores the broken places in your heart. Unpack your jumbled feelings through prayer, and let Him untangle them as you begin to understand each one.

Dear God, those panicky moments are terrible and destabilizing. My heart often feels as if it will beat right out of my chest. Let me feel Your peace-giving presence immediately. Amen.

DOING WHAT IS GOOD

Never let evil get the best of you;
instead, overpower evil with the good.
ROMANS 12:21 VOICE

At every turn, do good. Be a light in the darkness that points others to God's glory. Let your words bring encouragement to those around you, and let your actions be a beautiful and unexpected blessing. Consider that as believers we are God's ambassadors to share His kingdom with the world. If we decide to partner with the wrong things, they will eventually extinguish our light and our witness for others. They will remove our joy. And we'll be left parched and thirsty, trying to figure life out on our own.

One of the best ways to nurture healthy hearts is by connecting them to God's. Doing this allows us to love what He loves and hate what He hates, thus helping us to make better choices. Spiritual discernment through the Holy Spirit is a powerful tool that enables believers to see what is true and right with supernatural clarity. And this gives us the opportunity to turn others toward the Lord in meaningful ways by how we live each day.

Dear God, help me to be steadfast in my resolve so I'm able to choose good over evil in all matters. Keep me sharp and spiritually healthy as I walk out my faith imperfectly. And let Your Holy Spirit keep my eyes focused and my heart tender toward You always. Amen.

LISTENING AND OBEYING

Anyone who loves Me will listen to My voice and obey. The Father will love him, and We will draw close to him and make a dwelling place within him.

JOHN 14:23 VOICE

What we need more than anything else is Jesus. More than a good night's sleep—although it's wonderful when we get one—we need the Lord in our lives. More than a breather from busyness or a healthy eating and workout routine, a relationship with God tops the list. It's what will bring health to our body, soul, and mind.

Make sure you're listening as the Lord helps you navigate the mountain highs and valley lows, and then follow the path carved out for you. The Word is clear that our obedience results in blessings. So carve out time daily to spend in God's presence, reading the Bible, praying, and meditating on scripture. Draw close to Him when life feels overwhelming and you're running on fumes. Run to God for understanding when you can't untangle your feelings. Sit with Him in times of confusion and discouragement. Then you'll find comfort from His voice and strength to obey His leading.

Dear God, I do love You! Help me to listen to Your voice and obey what You tell me. I know that as I draw close to You, I will feel Your presence. More than anything, I need more of You in my life. Amen.

HONEST AND HEALTHY WORDS

Watch the way you talk. Let nothing foul or dirty come out of your mouth. Say only what helps, each word a gift.
EPHESIANS 4:29 MSG

Sometimes when we're weighed down by life, we aren't as mindful about our words as usual. Speaking with kindness and generosity isn't often at the top of our list when we are feeling swamped by to-dos. Instead, it's in those moments that we let unfiltered statements slip out. We become reckless with our remarks. And once those words are spoken, they can't be taken back. Just like toothpaste, once you squeeze it out of the tube, you can't push it back in.

When stressed out, be quick to ask God for discernment of what to say and what not to say. Ask Him for self-control so anxiety about an unrelated issue doesn't manifest as mean-spiritedness toward someone. And take inventory of your circumstances, trying to understand the reason for these feelings. Do you need to slow down? Press the PAUSE button? Rest? Reconnect with God? Let Him restore your worrisome heart so the words that flow from it can be honest and healthy.

Dear God, I confess there are times when I speak in unwholesome ways, and it's usually when I'm feeling overwhelmed by my circumstances. Help me stay in relationship with You, connecting in meaningful ways so I keep myself balanced. Amen.

THE WORTHLESS PURSUIT OF MONEY

"You cannot serve two masters: God and money. For you will hate one and love the other, or else the other way around."
MATTHEW 6:24 TLB

When in pursuit of money, we'll find ourselves compromising what we know is right. It becomes our master since we're often willing to do whatever is necessary to serve it. And at the end of the day, it'll leave us emotionally and spiritually bankrupt. We'll be unhealthy because we ignored divine warning signs telling us to reprioritize.

Do you fail to protect your schedule and instead work yourself to the bone? Rather than rest in the abundance of God's goodness, do you focus on all you're lacking? Have you sacrificed joy in hopes of a jet-setting lifestyle? Do you ignore what your spirit needs because you're busy chasing after the things of this world? Starting today, commit to choosing what is good and right. You can serve only one master: God or money. Let God be your life's pursuit, and watch how doing so yields abundant blessings that matter so much more than earthly riches.

Dear God, there are times I crave money over You. Forgive me for misguided priorities! Would You help me rearrange my heart so that I embrace eternal things over worldly ones? Help me want You over everything else. Amen.

GOD'S PEACE ISN'T FRAGILE

"I am leaving you with a gift—peace of mind and heart! And the peace I give isn't fragile like the peace the world gives. So don't be troubled or afraid."

JOHN 14:27 TLB

The world feels crazy right now. We're watching events play out that the Bible mentioned would eventually come to pass. We hear of wars and rumors of war. We're witnessing famines, plagues, and natural disasters. There is political unrest and confusion. And unless we keep our eyes on God, remembering He's on the throne and always will be, our hearts will be full of fear and worry.

But if instead we ask the Lord for His peace to rest on us, we'll be able to find comfort in the chaos. He will bring much-needed nourishment to our weary spirits. And while the world will offer plenty of ways to feel safe and secure, they will be subpar and short-lived. God's Word, however, says His peace is powerful and lasting, and it will rejuvenate your heart and restore your mind so you can stand strong no matter what comes your way.

Dear God, thank You for offering me the kind of peace that has weight and magnitude to it. I need it to calm my anxious heart. Please bring it right now and let me hold it tightly as I walk through unsettling times. Amen.

FAITHFULLY NOURISHING

Jesus replied, "'Love the Lord your God with all your heart, soul, and mind.'"
MATTHEW 22:37 TLB

Jesus said that to "love the Lord your God with all your heart, soul, and mind" is the first and greatest command of all time. And it's also one that's very difficult to walk out, especially when we're overly self-focused on getting through the day in one piece. As women, our to-do list is endless. From the moment our eyes open until the moment they close at night, we are moving from one task to the next. From getting kids to the places they need to be, to organizing the details of the home, to managing our own workflow . . .when do we have time to love God like today's verse commands?

Take this to the Lord in prayer. Ask Him to help you understand how to make this command a reality in your life. Let Him show you where to trim the fat off your schedule. Listen as He reveals how to be kinder to yourself. Do you need to reorganize some things? Friend, trust the Lord to show you how to live empowered and engaged while being faithful to nourish your relationship with Him daily.

Dear God, I'm at a loss for ways to be everything to everyone while keeping my eyes on You. Please show me how to glorify Your holy name today and always. Amen.

STAYING FOCUSED ON GOD

But Daniel determined that he would not defile himself by eating the king's food or drinking his wine, so he asked the head of the palace staff to exempt him from the royal diet.

DANIEL 1:8 MSG

While in exile in Babylon, Daniel resolved not to eat from the king's table. Why? As an Israelite living by the law, he knew the Babylonians' food consisted of unclean meat—the animals were improperly killed, and their food was considered contaminated since the first portion was offered to idols. Daniel also wanted to keep a clear mind, free of drunkenness by wine. He and his friends chose to honor God even in captivity, deciding to do nothing that might interfere with their physical, mental, and spiritual health.

Friend, how are you doing with this in your own life? In your busyness, are you staying focused on God above all else? Are you keeping true to His commands? Are you avoiding the contamination of the world? Like Daniel, are you keeping watch so that nothing interferes with your physical, mental, and spiritual health? Let's be the kind of women who stay true to what we know is good for us and bring glory to God.

Dear God, help me to be a modern-day Daniel in my resolve to let nothing derail me from following Your commands, for I know they bring life. Amen.

IT'S NOT ABOUT SELF-CENTEREDNESS

Don't let selfishness and prideful agendas take over. Embrace true humility, and lift your heads to extend love to others. Get beyond yourselves and protecting your own interests; be sincere, and secure your neighbors' interests first.

PHILIPPIANS 2:3–4 VOICE

Self-care doesn't mean self-centeredness. It's not about pushing others aside to ensure that all your needs are met. It's not ignoring family and friends and putting yourself first. Instead, it's about doing things God's way to ensure you're healthy so you can be a light in the world. The pursuit of emotional, spiritual, mental, and physical health is important so you can love others well. Perfection isn't the goal, but living with purpose is.

Too often we work at protecting our own interests at the expense of those around us. We see their needs. We hear about their struggles. But our prideful agendas keep our eyes on making ourselves happy first. Ask God to lift your head and open your eyes so you can stand strong with the hurting and hopeless. Be humble and honoring. Take care of yourself so you can take care of them.

Dear God, let me stay focused on my health because it will help me to be a blessing to those around me. Let the end goal of my self-care be selflessness. Amen.

WHY WE ACT LIKE BULLIES

Don't walk around with a chip on your shoulder, always spoiling for a fight. Don't try to be like those who shoulder their way through life. Why be a bully?
PROVERBS 3:30–31 MSG

When we act like bullies, it's often because we've hit our limit. Maybe we've been going ninety miles an hour and finally hit a brick wall. Maybe we've been running on fumes, trying to bring closure to a project. Maybe we have been carrying the lion's share of responsibilities at home for too long. And because our needs have been pushed to the bottom of the list, every bit of grace has been depleted.

Invite God into your hectic life and let Him help you reprioritize your schedule so you can breathe. If you ask, He will show you how to protect your schedule in smart ways. You'll learn how to press the PAUSE button so you don't burn out. Through His Spirit, you'll be proactive in taking care of your spiritual needs to keep you strong and wise. And as you choose to be kind to yourself in the right ways, grace will reappear. Joy will be restored. And you will be kind and generous toward others.

Dear God, I know I've had some rough edges lately. Forgive me for being a bully to those around me. Would You show me how to arrange my life in ways that will bless me and bring You glory? Amen.

TRYING TO GARNER ATTENTION

"And now about fasting. When you fast, declining your food for a spiritual purpose, don't do it publicly, as the hypocrites do, who try to look wan and disheveled so people will feel sorry for them. Truly, that is the only reward they will ever get."

MATTHEW 6:16 TLB

Many of us do things to garner attention. Can we just be honest about that? Whether we're on a rigid eating plan or working overtime to finish a project or volunteering long hours for a local charity, we often talk about it with selfish intentions. Maybe we want to be noticed and affirmed. Maybe we want pity. Or maybe we want to look selfless and self-sacrificing in the eyes of others. And while today's verse is talking specifically about fasting, the same concept holds true to other places in our lives.

Our journeys to healthy bodies, souls, and minds don't have to become public announcements, especially if we do so with wrong motives. There's no harm in sharing your new routine for accountability. Updating those interested is good too! But when you're hoping it will impress others and make you look better, let it be a red flag.

Dear God, I want my journey to a healthier me to be a humble one. Give me discernment to know when and if and with whom I should share. Amen.

OBEYING IN PRIVATE OR PUBLIC

So now, my beloved, obey as you have always done, not only when I am with you, but even more so when I can't be. Continue to work out your salvation, with great fear and trembling, because God is energizing you so that you will desire and do what always pleases Him.

PHILIPPIANS 2:12–13 VOICE

Are you the kind who follows the rules when others are watching but then relaxes when no one is around? We all have done this from time to time. We're imperfect, even when we try to live righteously. Amen? But let's never forget that God is always calling us higher. His desire is that we'll make choices that please Him when we're alone and in public.

Cutting corners will eventually come back to bite us. The Lord has prescribed a plan for your life that includes self-care. It's not about pampering but rather about purposeful living. It's taking care of yourself emotionally and spiritually. It's being good to your body and mind. It's caring for your heart. And all of this is so we can further His kingdom with the time we have on earth. So, obey the Lord always.

Dear God, let my greatest desire be to do what pleases You. Whether in private or in public, help me obey You with integrity so I can live out my best life and bring glory to Your name. Amen.

GOD'S KINDNESS

Because of his kindness, you have been saved through trusting Christ.
And even trusting is not of yourselves; it too is a gift from
God. Salvation is not a reward for the good we have
done, so none of us can take any credit for it.
EPHESIANS 2:8–9 TLB

God is kind to those who love Him. He's so kind, in fact, that He sent His one and only Son to die on a cross to pay the price for our sins—past, present, and future. It's through this act of love and not by anything we do that we are saved. We can't work our way to heaven by being good. But it's through God's grace that we can come to a saving faith in Jesus through trusting Him as our Savior.

When we choose to accept Christ, His light can be seen in us. The Holy Spirit within shines God's goodness into the world through our words and actions. In both good and hard times, faith helps us stay focused. It keeps us steady and balanced. And it's because of His kindness that we can rest, knowing that our imperfections have no bearing on our salvation.

Dear God, thank You for Jesus. Thank You for making a way to be with You in eternity that didn't require my works. That would have been a setup for failure. Help me trust in You every day and in every way. Amen.

THE PROBLEM WITH COMPLAINING

Do all things without complaining or bickering with each other, so you will be found innocent and blameless; you are God's children called to live without a single stain on your reputations among this perverted and crooked generation. Shine like stars across the land.

PHILIPPIANS 2:14–15 VOICE

The quickest way to kill any joy we have is to complain. When we focus on all that's wrong, it keeps us from seeing all that's right. And being grumpy and grouchy isn't an effective billboard for Christian living. Scripture says we're to shine like stars across the land. Choosing to have a cranky attitude effectively dims our shining ability. The light is still there—meaning we can't lose our salvation—but we're not glowing as brightly as possible.

Take inventory of your life. Are certain situations or people putting you in a bad mood? Is your calendar too full and you're exhausted? Are you spending time with God each day? Rather than complain to those around you, why not take those burdens to the Lord and ask for help? Let Him bring peace and comfort so you can take a deep breath. Let God remind You of His goodness in your life.

Dear God, help me stay positive, especially when I'm swamped by life's challenges. I don't want to complain to or about others. Instead, restore my heart so I can shine like a star across the land. Amen.

GOD MADE YOU ON PURPOSE

It is God himself who has made us what we are and given us new lives from Christ Jesus; and long ages ago he planned that we should spend these lives in helping others.
EPHESIANS 2:10 TLB

Today, let the words of Ephesians 2:10 ring true in your spirit, friend. God is your Creator, the one who made you special and unique. He is why we're all different in wonderful ways. God is the reason you have certain talents and those around you have different talents. You were made on purpose and for a purpose, just like everyone else. God thought you up, every detail. And God loves you with an unwavering love.

As you embark on practicing self-care, make sure your reasons are honest and honoring. Each decision you make to better yourself should be centered in the Lord and His will. It should be with His plans in mind. And it should be in an effort to shine His light in the world. Prioritize your emotional, physical, and spiritual health so you can love others while bringing glory to the Creator.

Dear God, thank You for making me the way You did, and forgive me for the times when I've tried to change myself for the wrong reasons. With this new life through Jesus, help me embrace my creation and calling so I can be a powerful witness for You here. Amen.

ONLY CARING ABOUT THEMSELVES

There is no one like Timothy. What sets him apart from others is his deep concern for you and your spiritual journey. This is rare, my friends, for most people only care about themselves, not about what is dear to the heart of Jesus the Anointed.

PHILIPPIANS 2:20–21 VOICE

In Paul's kind words about Timothy, he also gave a warning we should all heed. Did you see it? Paul talked about how so many people only care about themselves and what they need. They focus on what makes them happy, looking for ways to fulfill their selfish desires. Rather than opening their eyes to see the needs of others, the goal of the day is their own well-being. But Timothy exemplified the opposite, and Paul commended him for it.

It is important to be aware of our needs because ignoring them can eventually shut us down. Putting others first at the expense of our health can render us ineffective in the work God has called us to. So self-care is an important tool indeed. Ask God to lead you into nourishing practices so you're ready and able to walk out what is dear to His heart.

Dear God, help me find a delicate balance between caring for myself and loving on those around me. Let my motives for each be pure as I focus on what is important to You. Amen.

YOU BELONG

But now you belong to Christ Jesus, and though you once were far away from God, now you have been brought very near to him because of what Jesus Christ has done for you with his blood.

EPHESIANS 2:13 TLB

Sometimes we struggle to feel as if we belong. We feel excluded from groups we'd love to be part of. We feel unaccepted for what we believe or how we choose to live our lives. Can you relate? We all have a deep longing to fit in. There is something in each of us that wants to feel connected and valued. And many of us spend our lives trying to find that sacred space, often in unhealthy ways.

Friend, today's scripture clearly and powerfully tells us the truth. Are you listening? Once you become a believer in Jesus, you no longer have to hope for a sense of belonging. You belong. No more searching and hoping and longing for community. Because of Jesus' death on the cross, you have a place that cannot be taken away. And it's from this place that joy rises up and spills out into the world.

Dear God, thank You for bringing me into Your family through Jesus' sacrifice on the cross. Thank You for including me and loving me with unshakable love. And thank You that I am Yours forever. Amen.

GOD'S HOUSEHOLD

Now you are no longer strangers to God and foreigners to heaven, but you are members of God's very own family, citizens of God's country, and you belong in God's household with every other Christian.

EPHESIANS 2:19 TLB

In the previous devotional, I talked about the power of belonging. What a gift to know that God understands that basic need in us, so much so that He unpacks this concept throughout His Word, including in today's scripture passage. He wants us to wholeheartedly understand that we belong in His household. Once we surrender our hearts to Him by accepting Jesus as our Savior rather than relying on our own strength, we're brought into the fold of faith with other believers. How sweet that is.

This means we no longer must strive to fit in. We don't have to work ourselves to the bone to conform to the worldly standards of beauty or wealth. We can stop being our own harshest critics, pointing out the reasons we don't make the cut. Ask God to help you relax and embrace the truth that you belong in His household. You are now a member of God's family.

Dear God, thank You for bringing me into the fold of faith. Thank You for meeting the need for me to belong. What a privilege to be in Your family for all of eternity! Amen.

FRESH PRAYERS

"Don't recite the same prayer over and over as the heathen do, who think prayers are answered only by repeating them again and again. Remember, your Father knows exactly what you need even before you ask him!"

MATTHEW 6:7–8 TLB

Prayer should not be robotic or mechanical. Instead, God wants us to communicate sincerely with Him directly from our hearts. There is no reason to mindlessly repeat prayers, because He already knows what we need before we ask. We don't need the perfect words or eloquent phrases, because prayer isn't a magical incantation. When we talk to God, it should be an expression of the heart. Let's choose to be women who understand the weight of prayer as we talk to Him with fresh and honest feelings.

A healthy prayer life is important to nurture. That time in God's presence will bring about joy and peace. It will usher in wisdom and discernment. Prayer will comfort your weary heart and bring a much-needed divine perspective. And it will give you a safe place to be honest with the one who can save, heal, and restore.

Dear God, help my prayers to be fresh and authentic. Let me steer clear of the same words or phrases so talking with You doesn't become emotionless. Instead, bring my prayer time to life so it becomes a joyful expression of my love for You. Amen.

GROWING IN THE FAITH

For you are still only baby Christians, controlled by your own desires, not God's. When you are jealous of one another and divide up into quarreling groups, doesn't that prove you are still babies, wanting your own way? In fact, you are acting like people who don't belong to the Lord at all.

1 CORINTHIANS 3:3 TLB

As believers, we are expected to grow in faith daily. Not only will we crave spiritual progress, but we'll also take the next steps to make that happen. We'll go from milk to meat and potatoes as we mature. By spending time in God's Word, talking with Him in prayer, and being in fellowship with others, we will grow. And with that comes a shift in how we walk out our faith.

But when our main focus is ourselves, we will become self-absorbed. We'll battle to get what we want. We'll position ourselves above others. And rather than stand in solidarity with others, we'll see the places where we're lacking as we battle jealousy. Ask God to grow you up in faith so your heart is healthy and able to be confident and loving.

Dear God, give me the desire to develop my faith in meaningful and important ways. Let my words and actions prove I am Yours, keeping me from getting caught up in selfishness, jealousy, and fighting. Amen.

CLINGING TO JOY

The thief approaches with malicious intent, looking to steal, slaughter, and destroy; I came to give life with joy and abundance.

JOHN 10:10 VOICE

If you're lacking joy, let it be a red flag that something is wrong. We know from today's scripture that a life spent with Jesus brings joy to the believer. It brings abundance in the places needed. This doesn't mean life will be easy and pain-free, but the Lord will lead us through by His goodness and love.

Scripture is also clear that the enemy's plans are to crush those who follow Jesus. He comes to steal, slaughter, and destroy our heart and hopes. He wants to ruin everything, bringing deep discouragement as often as possible. And too often, friend, he succeeds.

Choose today to stand in God's strength and cling to the joy Jesus came to give. Let not your heart be troubled for He is with you. He sees your challenges and has made a way through them. Ask God to reignite joy so it shines from you no matter the difficult circumstances. With Him, both can exist at the same time.

Dear God, I want to fully embrace a life with joy and abundance. I want to be so enamored with You that the enemy can't find a way to turn my heart from being dependent on and expectant for Your goodness. Amen.

IGNORING WORLDLY STANDARDS

Stop fooling yourselves. If you count yourself above average in intelligence, as judged by this world's standards, you had better put this all aside and be a fool rather than let it hold you back from the true wisdom from above.

1 CORINTHIANS 3:18 TLB

Who cares about what the world thinks is good and right? Who cares about the standards it creates to judge the worthiness of people? Why do we give an ounce of concern about following the world's ways when we know there is nothing eternal for us here? And why do we strive to be who the world says is important when doing so is in the opposite direction of God? Let's stop being fools, friend.

The only reason we should be concerned about self-care is because it keeps us healthy to do the Lord's work on earth. It's not about fitting in or living up to earthly expectations. Instead, it's about being ready to love others as we further His kingdom. We should seek His wisdom, not our own. We should lean on His discernment each day. And we should turn a deaf ear to the world because no true wisdom is found in it. Be diligent to stay emotionally, physically, and spiritually healthy so you're able to walk out the wonderful plans God has in store for your life.

Dear God, help me keep my eyes on You alone, not getting caught up in worldly standards. Amen.

THE NEED FOR REST

Then Jesus suggested, "Let's get away from the crowds for a while and rest." For so many people were coming and going that they scarcely had time to eat. So they left by boat for a quieter spot.

MARK 6:31–32 TLB

Recognize that even Jesus needed to rest. In His divinity, there would be no need. But walking the earth as a human allowed Jesus to experience all that we do, including the need to take a breather. Too often we find ourselves running at a breakneck pace. Our day becomes a blur as we go from one crazy moment to the next. And once our feet hit the floor in the morning, our day of insanity begins.

Think about it. What keeps you from making the right choices to better protect your schedule? Why won't you take time to rest, especially in hectic seasons? What keeps you from pressing the PAUSE button, giving yourself a much-needed moment to regroup mentally and physically? Maybe it's because you're afraid to let others down. Do you feel guilty for saying no? Are you afraid of missing out? It's important we listen to God's prompting to be kinder to ourselves and rest. Is He trying to get your attention?

Dear God, help me know when my body and mind need rest. And give me the courage and wisdom to make it happen. Amen.

FOR THE NEXT GENERATION

What strikes me most is how natural and sincere your faith is. I am convinced that the same faith that dwelt in your grandmother, Lois, and your mother, Eunice, abides in you as well.

2 TIMOTHY 1:5 VOICE

If there was ever a power-packed reason to keep yourself spiritually healthy, it's knowing that spiritual health can be passed on to the next generation. What a privilege to effectively share our love for the Lord with our children and grandchildren and watch it take root in their hearts. Is there any better gift we could give them?

Let this be the encouragement you need to dig deeper into your relationship with God. Be intentional to grow your faith by setting aside time each day to spend with Him. Open the Bible and read it, meditating on scripture as God leads. Get on your knees and pour out your heart to Him. Let Him hear your praises and problems in equal measure. And watch as the Lord nourishes your soul, giving you the testimony that will infiltrate the lives of those around you with power and might.

Dear God, I love knowing that my faith can positively affect my children and their children. That's a generational blessing that will reap goodness for years to come. Thank You for honoring my faith by passing it on in meaningful ways. Amen.

AN EXPERT IN MULTIPLYING

He took the five loaves and two fish and looking up to heaven, gave thanks for the food. Breaking the loaves into pieces, he gave some of the bread and fish to each disciple to place before the people. And the crowd ate until they could hold no more!

MARK 6:41–42 TLB

We serve a God of abundance, and the good news is that He can do so much with so little. When life has beaten you down and you're desperate for His help, all you need is a mustard seed of faith. When you are struggling to find joy in the hardships, your small hope in the Lord will be multiplied. With just a little flicker of light, God can ignite your heart to be a light in the darkness. If He can feed a crowd of five thousand with five small loaves of barley bread and two fish, you can trust that He has you covered.

Where are you feeling depleted today? Where does it seem you're lacking? In what areas of your life are you worried that you're not enough? Friend, God is an expert in multiplying. He can take your ordinary and make it extraordinary. He can increase your joy, brighten your light, and feed your soul. Trust the Lord to encourage and strengthen you to walk in victory. He's the only one who can.

Dear God, bring increase in my life as You see fit. Amen.

IT'S NOT ABOUT SELF-PROMOTION

"But when you do a kindness to someone, do it secretly—
don't tell your left hand what your right hand is doing.
And your Father, who knows all secrets, will reward you."
MATTHEW 6:3–4 TLB

Self-care should not include self-promotion. Do the important things that nourish your soul, but don't brag about them. Don't serve others hoping it elevates their opinion of you. Don't be sacrificial because you want others to acknowledge your sacrifice. God wants us to rest from that kind of striving and be kind simply because doing so blesses the intended and brings God glory. He sees the heart. Let's make sure we pour into others with authenticity and humility.

Who in your community needs to be blessed? Who could use a pick-me-up that brings joy? Where can you shine God's goodness into another's life by loving on them with intention? Let the Lord direct as you stay open to being kind and generous. Let Him use your hands and feet as His. And then keep it between you and God, for He will bless your discretion.

Dear God, forgive me for the times I've done things to get attention. Forgive me for the times I've been generous only because I wanted it to reflect well on me. Moving forward, let me be Your hands and feet to those You put before me, loving on them in secret simply because You asked and they needed it. Amen.

NOT A COWARDLY SPIRIT

This is why I write to remind you to stir up the gift of God that was conveyed to you when I laid my hands upon you. You see, God did not give us a cowardly spirit but a powerful, loving, and disciplined spirit.
2 TIMOTHY 1:6–7 VOICE

You are a strong woman of God simply because of the gifts God has given you. You may feel weak at times, unable to muster strength for the exhausting circumstances you're having to navigate. You might not have all the answers to life's difficult challenges. You may be running on empty, desperate for a break from everyone pulling on you. You may even feel that life is out of control and you're unsure how to make it manageable once again. But, friend, God has given you an internal strength that you can access at any time.

In those times when you don't feel equipped to care for your own needs, remember that God has you covered. He has thought of everything. You may feel weak and fainthearted. You may feel spineless to step up. But God didn't give that kind of spirit to you. Instead, you've been given one of power, love, and self-control.

Dear God, thank You for giving me a spirit that can stand strong and resolved when life gets messy. I'm so thankful You've thought of everything. Amen.

TRAINED FOR HOLY LIVING

Train yourself for a holy life! While physical training has some value, training in holy living is useful for everything. It has promise for this life now and the life to come.

1 TIMOTHY 4:7–8 CEB

Let part of your self-care routine include training for holy living. While we often make physical and emotional health a priority, spiritual health can sometimes slip through the cracks. We forget how valuable it can be as we're trying to navigate the mountain highs and valley lows life brings our way. And while it's important to have a strong body and mind, we're at a deficit without the pursuit of holy living.

How do we train for it? Simply put, we find ways to connect to the heart of God. Because when we do, it will prompt us to love what He loves and hate what He hates. It will give us strength to make choices that are good for us and glorify Him. And it will inspire our greatest desire to be sharing God's goodness to the world in profound and significant ways.

Dear God, thank You for the reminder that my spiritual health is essential for holy living. When I forgo that pursuit, it weakens me in every way because I need Your power to walk out this life with strength and wisdom. Train me up in holiness. I want more of You. Amen.

GOD IS THE ONE WHO SAVES

God is the one who saved and called us with a holy calling. This wasn't based on what we have done, but it was based on his own purpose and grace that he gave us in Christ Jesus before time began.

2 TIMOTHY 1:9 CEB

The world is full of reminders that we need to work harder. We feel the need to work faster and smarter. We are encouraged to push every boundary so we come out on top and succeed. One look at our calendars would show clear confirmation of this. Because failure is not an option, we want to push ourselves with gusto. In the end, we're exhausted, cranky, and overwhelmed. And even with our best effort and diligence, we still fail at times.

When it comes to salvation, however, there's nothing we can do to earn it. We don't have to work at it or be strategic. It's not something we can produce in our own strength or lose in our imperfection. Prioritizing our physical, emotional, or mental health can't bring it about. God is the one who called us to Him through Jesus. You can rest in that beautiful truth today.

Dear God, what a gift to be called by You and saved by Jesus. It's a gift to know there's nothing I can do to earn it or lose it. At every turn You bless me. Thank You. Amen.

AGE DOESN'T MATTER

Don't let anyone look down on you because you are young. Instead, set an example for the believers through your speech, behavior, love, faith, and by being sexually pure.

1 TIMOTHY 4:12 CEB

You don't have to be a seasoned woman to make a difference. Not all wisdom comes with age. Some have lived a lifetime before they even hit forty. So don't count yourself out of mentoring based on how many years you've lived on planet Earth. In so many ways, it just doesn't matter.

To those younger women committed to being spiritually healthy, you're often wiser than those who are older because you've allowed the Lord to grow you up in the faith. Each time you prayed for wisdom and discernment, it showed. Opening your Bible to search for answers to life's troubles made a difference. Every investment in maturing your faith added depth to your walk with God. And, friend, rest knowing your life sets an example for others in powerful ways. They see your journey with Jesus, and He has used it to encourage and challenge, often without you even knowing it. Well done.

Dear God, thank You for allowing my life to make a difference regardless of my age. Help me continue to grow in You so I can be a source of encouragement to those around me. Let my life's journey point others to You. Amen.

SUFFERING

This is also why I'm suffering the way I do, but I'm not ashamed. I know the one in whom I've placed my trust. I'm convinced that God is powerful enough to protect what he has placed in my trust until that day.

2 TIMOTHY 1:12 CEB

Suffering is part of life. And while no one enjoys those seasons, the truth is that they create powerful testimonies through us. Walking out a life of faith is both beautiful and challenging. It takes all you have to cling to the Lord when storms hit. Scripture is crystal clear that we will have struggles as we navigate the highs and lows of our time on earth. But we can hold our heads up because we have God. We can trust Him fully and completely each day and in every circumstance.

Overcoming does, however, require us to press into our relationships with Him. We must be spiritually healthy to withstand tough times. So let that be part of your self-care routine. Without a firm foundation of faith and an ongoing connection with the Father, suffering will be unbearable. But with Him, you'll be protected as you let your life preach of God's goodness as you trust and believe.

Dear God, I know I will suffer, and You will hold me through it. Let my testimony through the storms speak loudly. Amen.

ONLY HIS OPINION

Here's whose opinion you should be concerned about: the One who can take your life and then throw you into hell! He's the only One you should fear! But don't misunderstand: you don't really need to be afraid of God, because God cares for every little sparrow. How much is a sparrow worth—don't five of them sell for a few cents?

LUKE 12:5–6 VOICE

Too often we get hung up on what others think of us. We care too much about their opinions, and that becomes an obsession. We want to be liked. We want to be affirmed and accepted. And eventually, pleasing others becomes all we worry about. But scripture says the only opinion we should care about is God's. Friend, do you ever think about that?

When the Bible tells us to *fear* God, it means to have deep reverence and awe. Our desire each day should be to live in ways that please Him, not others. We should spend time nourishing our souls in His Word. We should pray for overflowing joy so we live in victory. And we should do the things that keep our light shining brightly for the Lord. He loves and cares for us, and we can lean into Him for what we need to glorify His name.

Dear God, let Your opinion be the only one that matters to me. Amen.

HE WILL CARRY OUR BURDENS

"Come to me and I will give you rest—all of you who work so hard beneath a heavy yoke. Wear my yoke—for it fits perfectly—and let me teach you; for I am gentle and humble, and you shall find rest for your souls; for I give you only light burdens."

MATTHEW 11:28–30 TLB

Let God be the one to carry your burdens. As women, we're used to putting the weight of the world on our shoulders and going about trying to manage each task with excellence. We feel capable, and so we forgo asking for help. We can multitask with the best of them, can't we? But in the end, it proves to be too much. Rather than stand strong, we buckle under the pressure. We wilt in our own strength, and we always will.

Friend, what heavy burden are you carrying today? What is bogging you down with anxiety and stress? The best self-care practice we can embrace is letting God carry the burdens that bring discouragement. When we become unbalanced, He will strengthen us physically, emotionally, mentally, and spiritually. Yes, God will give you rest to restore your soul and bring you hope.

Dear God, help me trust You when life feels too big. Help me give You everything that weighs me down. Amen.

THE NUMBER OF HAIRS

Since you are so much more precious to God than a thousand flocks of sparrows, and since God knows you in every detail—down to the number of hairs on your head at this moment—you can be secure and unafraid of any person, and you have nothing to fear from God either.

LUKE 12:7 VOICE

Knowing that God has every hair on your head numbered should reveal how very much you matter to Him. Let the truth of His deep love and adoration nourish your soul today. He understands the details of all that's discouraging you right now. He sees the complexity of your emotions and grasps the complications they bring. God appreciates the load you've been carrying, recognizing how it's affecting you in the day-to-day. And while He has already made a way for you to get through the storm safely, the Lord promises to walk with you each step until that comes to pass. Why? Because you are so precious to Him.

Don't try to go through life without the Lord. There's no need to go it alone, especially because you're deeply loved. And as believers, we have access to the Father for every need that arises, be it emotional, physical, or spiritual. You have nothing to fear.

Dear God, knowing how much I matter to You fills me with joy. Amen.

CHOOSING YOUR ATTITUDE

A happy heart is good medicine and a joyful mind causes healing, but a broken spirit dries up the bones.

PROVERBS 17:22 AMP

We must choose our attitudes rather than let our emotions dictate how we act and feel. We may have had a crummy day, but we cannot take it out on those we love. We may be in a very difficult season of marriage or overwhelmed in parenting, but it's important we stay balanced. Even if our health is challenging, our financial situation seems dire, or we're struggling with personal trauma, as believers we can have happy hearts and joyful minds. God is what makes that possible. He is why we're able to stand in victory and choose to stay expectant.

In those tough moments when we feel dried up, be intentional to remember all the Lord has done for you. Replay the times you've seen His goodness in life. And let those memories lighten your heart and bring healing to your soul. Rather than partner with doom and despair, pray to feel God's presencc. Ask for supernatural peace and comfort. Ask Him to bring joy overflowing. And as you wait, do so with great expectation because You know He will show up in meaningful ways.

Dear God, help me live with great expectation, for You are a good Father! Amen.

HONEST ABOUT SHORTCOMINGS

If we go around bragging, "We have no sin," then we are fooling ourselves and are strangers to the truth. But if we own up to our sins, God shows that He is faithful and just by forgiving us of our sins and purifying us from the pollution of all the bad things we have done.

1 JOHN 1:8–9 VOICE

Friend, it's okay not to be perfect. Rest assured that God has no expectation we will be. So choose to be honest about every shortcoming. Embrace the truth of your limitations. Admit weaknesses. Any tendency to present ourselves as blameless—be it to God or others—is not authentic. It's not true. And it puts undue pressure on us to strive for greatness rather than to trust the Lord.

When we own up to our inadequacies, consider how it brightens the light that shines from within us. It lets others see our faithfulness as we trust God to make up the difference when our humanity falls short. It highlights His power and might as they watch Him fill in the gaps each time we fail. And it keeps us humble and dependent on God for our emotional and spiritual health because we know we can't nourish our souls without Him.

Dear God, thank You for loving me despite my shortcomings. Amen.

HE WILL GIVE YOU WORDS

Don't worry how you'll respond, and don't worry what you should say. The Holy Spirit will give you the words to say at the moment when you need them.

LUKE 12:11–12 VOICE

When we're poised to have hard conversations, we often worry about finding the right words to speak. We stress about getting our words right and having impactful responses that are received well. But when we get all stirred up about it, we're forgetting the Spirit's role in our words. When we became believers, God gave us His Holy Spirit to live inside us and guide us. He leads us by faith if we'll listen and obey. And today's verse reminds us that the Spirit will put words in our mouths when we need them.

Rest in that promise today. Let it settle your anxious heart. Your job is to stay connected to the Lord so your soul is fed with His goodness. You're to lean into Him through prayer, knowing these difficult conversations will happen. And then watch as the words come so you can speak with God's power and might backing them up. It's your pursuit of spiritual health that will usher in what you need in the moment.

Dear God, let me rest in Your promise of the right words at the right time. Amen.

PROTECTING YOUR RELATIONSHIPS

He who covers and forgives an offense seeks love, but he who repeats or gossips about a matter separates intimate friends.

PROVERBS 17:9 AMP

Be kind to yourself by protecting the relationships God blesses you with. It's not always easy to do, but it's important. God is for community, and He gives us a robust group of family and friends so we can walk through life together, supporting one another through challenges and celebrations. Community is a gift, one we're to nurture with great intentionality.

While all relationships ebb and flow, God knows that gossip has the power to bring irreconcilable separation. Today's verse tells us to be careful with how we handle unflattering news we hear about others or experience ourselves. Rather than expose the sordid details to someone else, we're told to cover it. If necessary, go directly to the person. But friendship brings a sweetness to our lives that ushers in joy, helps us understand our feelings, and nourishes our souls. When we do anything to damage it, it's not only an unkind act toward them but also to us.

Dear God, help me steward relationships with love and forgiveness. Help me remember the gift they are, even when messy at times. And give me the strength to care for them, recognizing the beautiful value they hold. Amen.

STAY ON GUARD

Most importantly, be disciplined and stay on guard. Your enemy the devil is prowling around outside like a roaring lion, just waiting and hoping for the chance to devour someone.
1 PETER 5:8 VOICE

One reason it's important to take care of ourselves is because when we're tired and overwhelmed, we often let our guard down. In those times, we are so desperate for downtime and nothingness that we're like sitting ducks. We're an easy catch, so to speak. And scripture is clear about the need to be watchful. Why? Because we have an enemy who is looking for ways to wreak havoc in our lives every day, so making sure we're mentally, emotionally, and spiritually healthy is important.

Knowing that, what changes do you need to make? Maybe you should do a better job of protecting your schedule so you're finding time for what reenergizes you. Maybe you need to take a moment to evaluate the situation, deciding if the next right step is carrying on or stopping. Maybe it's about resting rather than running at a breakneck pace. Regardless, there is great value in finding the right balance so you can be disciplined and stay on guard.

Dear God, help me care for myself so I'm able to be watchful. I don't want to be so preoccupied with my life that I fail to see the enemy's plans. Amen.

WE HAVE ENOUGH

Speaking to the people, he went on, "Take care! Protect yourself against the least bit of greed. Life is not defined by what you have, even when you have a lot."

LUKE 12:15 MSG

Sometimes we don't even realize we're in a rat race with those around us. Why? Because it's been a part of our lives as far back as we can remember and we're desensitized to it. Chances are we've been conditioned since childhood to want more or better, even if what we have is enough. And it's exhausting.

There is a remedy, and it's called faith. The more time we spend digging into the Word and letting each verse wash over us, the more we'll realize how wealthy we really are. The Bible will help us understand the riches that are ours through the blessing of Jesus. It will make the things of this world grow strangely dim in the most wonderful ways. And rather than be fixated on accumulating stuff to keep up with others, we'll experience contentment and peace. We will hunger for more of God, which will feed our souls and focus our desires on Him alone. We will discover that He is enough!

Dear God, I confess that jealousy and greed are a struggle at times. Help me keep my eyes on what matters most—You! Amen.

HE CAN LIGHTEN THE LOAD

Since God cares for you, let Him carry all your burdens and worries.
1 PETER 5:7 VOICE

Worry seems to be part of our DNA. We worry about our marriages, our kids, our finances, our aging parents, our careers, our reputations, and a million other things. But it's not that we like to worry. We don't look for things to be worried about. We aren't hoping to fill our days (and often nights) with it either. But many of us understand the massive role it plays in our lives, whether we want it to or not. So what can we do to lighten the load we carry? Pray.

Friend, God never designed us to handle life on our own. We can't, though we try! He gave us a big heart to love others, but we weren't created to carry the burdens that come with those relationships. We don't always have the answers for the issues that plague us. Let's remember this, because if ignored, we will be crushed under the weight of worry. Our hearts will be filled with anxiety and stress and fear. But when we choose to spend time with God daily, letting Him bring much-needed nourishment to our souls, we'll be able to strike the perfect balance between what we pick up and what we put down.

Dear God, thank You for carrying my burdens and worries. Amen.

TRUST AND NOT WORRY

Then turning to his disciples he said, "Don't worry about whether you have enough food to eat or clothes to wear. . . . Look at the ravens—they don't plant or harvest or have barns to store away their food, and yet they get along all right—for God feeds them. And you are far more valuable to him than any birds!"

LUKE 12:22, 24 TLB

When we feel lacking, we often go into panic mode and try to figure out solutions on our own. We worry about paying our bills because we understand the consequences if we don't. We stress about feeding our families and the ability to provide for what they may need. Our car may be acting up or we may need costly medical attention. But rather than us carrying the burden these things bring us, God wants us to flex our trust muscle.

Here's the problem: Unless we build that muscle up through time in the Word and prayer, it won't be there when we need it. We simply won't have the strength necessary to withstand the storms of life. Our faith won't be secure enough to point us toward God. And rather than rest in Him, believing He will meet our every need in perfect timing, we will flounder when our humanity reaches its limits. The Lord says not to worry but to trust. Let's do that.

Dear God, grow my faith so I can trust You with all things without question. Amen.

BE A BLESSING

The beginning of strife is like letting out water [as from a small break in a dam; first it trickles and then it gushes]; therefore abandon the quarrel before it breaks out and tempers explode.

PROVERBS 17:14 AMP

Taking care of our bodies and minds helps us stay levelheaded. Being smart about how we fill each day helps us strike the right balance so we stay grounded. But when we aren't letting God lead our schedules, crankiness and crabbiness often flow from it.

Are you good about inviting the Lord into your calendar planning? Do you pray about taking on new commitments before you make a move? Do you listen to the Holy Spirit prompting you to slow down or stop altogether? Are you spending time with God, letting Him nourish your parched soul daily? Are you mindful of healthy foods and exercise? Friend, every time you make an investment in the right things, doing so allows you to be a blessing to others rather than a bother.

Dear God, show me Your plan for each of my days so I can bless from obedience rather than curse from exhaustion. Help me make the right time investments with You at the lead. Help me to take care of my body and mind. Amen.

GOD FULLY UNDERSTANDS

After you have suffered for a little while, the God of grace who has called you [to His everlasting presence] through Jesus the Anointed will restore you, support you, strengthen you, and ground you.

1 PETER 5:10 VOICE

What a blessing to know that God fully understands what you are feeling. Down to the very core, He gets it. He has complete knowledge of each detail and wholly grasps the complexity of the emotions overwhelming you right now. God sees your suffering and allows it only because He'll work the pain for your good and His glory. And scripture reminds us that this season won't last forever.

Ask the Lord to help you work through the difficulties. Let Him help you better appreciate the range of emotions you're having to navigate. Spend time in prayer and watch how He brings fresh revelation. Dig into God's Word and see the ways you begin to understand the ins and outs of your feelings. Through every trial and challenge, God promises to restore, support, strengthen, and ground you.

Dear God, I love that You have full knowledge of everything I feel. You understand every detail with crisp clarity. In those times when I try to hide away from the hard seasons, remind me that I am safe in Your capable hands and that Your promise to be with me each step of the way is immovable. Amen.

STRIPPING OFF

Since we have such a huge crowd of men of faith watching us from the grandstands, let us strip off anything that slows us down or holds us back, and especially those sins that wrap themselves so tightly around our feet and trip us up; and let us run with patience the particular race that God has set before us.

HEBREWS 12:1 TLB

What a beautiful image we see from today's verse. We're being called to "strip off" the things that slow us down or hold us back from living a fully faith-filled life. Whatever might cause us to trip up, we're to remove. We are to get rid of the struggles and sins that tightly wrap around us. Take time today to consider what these may be in your life.

Are you too busy—do you pack your day from sunup to sundown? Are you guarding a secret sin that's rotting you from the inside out? Is an addiction running your life, keeping you enslaved and unhappy? Is the light of Jesus inside you growing dim from continual bad choices? Ask God to bring healing and restoration to your soul. Let Him reignite your joy. And from that, run the race the Lord has set before you!

Dear God, I don't want anything to keep me from following Your perfect plan for my life. Amen.

STRENGTH OVER SPINELESSNESS

If you want to keep from becoming fainthearted and weary,
think about [Jesus'] patience as sinful men did such terrible things to him.
HEBREWS 12:3 TLB

Jesus showed great patience as He endured the cross. He knew the joy that would come later because of His perseverance to stick with God's plan. And that understanding allowed Jesus a unique perspective to stand strong and undergo all that came at Him. We may not be able to see God's plan like He did, but we can trust our faithful Father to be with us each step of the way. That alone is why we can keep from becoming weary in our struggles. It's why we can have joy in hardship.

Are you feeling bogged down by life and filled with worry? Are you afraid you won't be able to suffer and stand? Jesus may have been divine, but on earth He was fully human, subjected to every mortal feeling and emotion. And if He was able to endure, with His help, so can you. Friend, just as Jesus trusted the Father to empower Him to persevere, He will do the same for you. Put your trust in God, because you'll receive strength over spinelessness and courage over cowardice.

Dear God, help me cling to You in the hard times. And as encouragement, help me remember that Jesus, in His humanness, endured with patience. With Your help, I can too. Amen.

WHAT'S THE USE OF WORRYING?

"And besides, what's the use of worrying? What good does it do? Will it add a single day to your life? Of course not! And if worry can't even do such little things as that, what's the use of worrying over bigger things?"
LUKE 12:25–26 TLB

Luke 12:25–26 is one of those passages of scripture that makes us yell, "Hallelujah!" one second and then shudder as we try to walk it out the next. We may pump our fist in the air in staunch agreement but fall short the next moment. As women, we desperately want this to be our way of living yet struggle to walk it out every day. Sometimes it seems there's just too much to worry about. And when we're scared for our marriage, stressed in parenting, concerned about our health, anxious about making ends meet financially, how can we not worry?

Scripture isn't making light of what burdens us. These verses aren't trivializing our struggles. Instead, they are meant to remind us to lean heavily on God because what's stealing our joy isn't worth it. Instead, let's give it all to God. Let's unload it every time we feel the weight of it. And when we do, joy and peace will wash over our worrisome hearts.

Dear God, take every burden that sits on me today and exchange it for Your peace and love. Amen.

BEING TRAINED BY GOD

Let God train you, for he is doing what any loving father does for his children. Whoever heard of a son who was never corrected? If God doesn't punish you when you need it, as other fathers punish their sons, then it means that you aren't really God's son at all—that you don't really belong in his family.

HEBREWS 12:7–8 TLB

At times the Lord must discipline those He loves. While none of us enjoys those moments, they are necessary and reveal His deep love. And because God is God, we can trust that His correction won't fill us with shame and guilt. We won't be condemned or left to feel attacked. Instead, the Lord's correction will help us see our need for Him, and we will be encouraged to make changes so our light will shine brightly again.

Scripture says we need to let God train us up in the right ways so we can thrive. When we live in our own understanding and follow our own paths, our journeys will be littered with bad decisions and natural consequences. But each time we choose God, our hearts will be full of joy, and we'll find peace no matter what life brings our way.

Dear God, I submit to You and Your training. Open my eyes to reveal parts of my life that need help and healing. I trust You. Amen.

SEEKING HIS PLAN

People do their best making plans for their lives,
but the Eternal guides each step.
PROVERBS 16:9 VOICE

Understanding the role God plays in guiding our daily journey is a gift. As believers, we're to seek His plan for our lives. We should be asking the Lord for clarity on our next steps. We should set before Him big decisions, waiting for answers. Our small, everyday choices should include Him too. And as we move forward, let it be in faith based on what we feel God is telling us to do. We can then trust that, if necessary, our course will be corrected at the right time and in the right ways. In other words, we can confidently err on the side of faith because the Lord will either confirm or redirect.

As scripture directs, let's do our very best to make plans that will benefit us and glorify God. The Holy Spirit will help us stay on the right track if we will listen. Let's bathe each day in prayer and ask for divine direction throughout the day. Be it in relationships, work, health, finances, or at a personal crossroad, let's be wise in how we proceed.

Dear God, nourish my soul with Your love and compassion to keep me headed in the right direction. I want to follow Your perfect plan for my life. Amen.

A CLEAN AND HOLY LIFE

Try to stay out of all quarrels, and seek to live a clean and holy life, for one who is not holy will not see the Lord. Look after each other so that not one of you will fail to find God's best blessings. Watch out that no bitterness takes root among you, for as it springs up it causes deep trouble, hurting many in their spiritual lives.

HEBREWS 12:14–15 TLB

The pursuit of living a clean and holy life helps our light shine brighter for others to see. As we try to stay free from quarreling, others will take notice. As we refuse to let bitterness take root, others will take note of our demeanor. And our hope should be that the intentional choices we make to love God with all our hearts, minds, and souls will help them find Jesus too. Caring for our spiritual health will have an impact on theirs as well.

So, knowing this, what changes do you need to make in how you're living right now? Where do you need to apply more effort to embrace a clean and holy life? Is anger or bitterness slowly creeping in? Ask God to help you keep the light aflame and visible to the dark world around you.

Dear God, guide me as I pursue clean and holy living. Let my life point others to You. Amen.

WALK AS THE WISE

So be careful how you live; be mindful of your steps. Don't run around like idiots as the rest of the world does. Instead, walk as the wise! Make the most of every living and breathing moment because these are evil times. So understand and be confident in God's will, and don't live thoughtlessly.

EPHESIANS 5:15–17 VOICE

This life in relation to eternity is but a breath. Our time here is short. So let's embrace it and be mindful of our steps, just as the Lord suggests. Let's make them intentional rather than reckless. Let's make choices that are good for our physical health, like resting and pressing PAUSE when necessary. Let's be authentic before God in prayer and consistent in reading His Word so our spiritual health stays strong. And let's invest time to better understand our feelings and find ways to be kinder to ourselves so our emotional health won't suffer. These will help us walk as the wise!

Too many people, even believers, squander their time with meaningless things. They get wrapped up in worldly offerings and lost in all the wrong things, and life passes them by. Rather than follow God's path for their lives, they walk in selfishness. Let's stay connected to the Lord, for doing so will give us the tools we need to be thoughtful in the here and now.

Dear God, help me to be mindful of my steps. Amen.

AS WE SHOULD

Teach us to number our days and recognize how few they are; help us to spend them as we should.

PSALM 90:12 TLB

When the Bible says we should spend our days here on earth "as we should," what does that mean? It means receiving God's kindness so we can live with constant joy. It's asking God to replace our misery with gladness and evil with goodness. It's looking for His hand to bring forth miracles so all can see His glory on display in our lives. It's living in ways that bring God's favor so we can experience success. It's spending time in His presence so our light shines, pointing others to the Father in heaven.

Friend, the desire to care for ourselves should only be because we want to spend our days here "as we should." Let it not be for vain purposes. Let it not be for selfish reasons. Let it not be driven by jealousy and envy or the desire to stay relevant or become important. God numbered our days because it's the time we needed to follow His plan for our lives. So let's choose to focus on self-care so we can be full of passion and perseverance, making our days here matter.

Dear God, help me spend my time on earth in ways that glorify Your holy name to those around me. Amen.

HE WILL ALWAYS GIVE. . .IF

"All mankind scratches for its daily bread, but your heavenly Father knows your needs. He will always give you all you need from day to day if you will make the Kingdom of God your primary concern."

LUKE 12:30–31 TLB

God isn't a magic genie who works to please us. We can't rub the Bible and expect God to pop out and give us our heart's desire. Nor is the Lord subservient, waiting like a Labrador retriever for us to tell Him what to do next. But God does love us unconditionally. He is fully aware of our needs and will meet them all. The Lord knows what is best. He always has the perfect timing. And He promises to take care of us according to His will. But, friend, did you catch our role in this beautiful pledge?

Today's passage makes an important clarification for believers. It's key because it triggers God's goodness to flow into your neediest places. He says He'll *always* give *all* we need *if* we make Him our primary concern. If we seek to nourish our souls through prayer and time in the Bible. If we obey His commands with joy and gladness. If we seek Him over everything else every day. If we make God number one, He will respond in powerful ways to our needs.

Dear God, help me put You first because I love You. And thank You that my pursuit will bring blessings. Amen.

NEVER GIVE UP

And let us not get tired of doing what is right, for after a while we will reap a harvest of blessing if we don't get discouraged and give up.
GALATIANS 6:9 TLB

It's so easy to get discouraged when we're trying to do what's right. Maybe our efforts are not being well received and we're losing motivation. Maybe we feel too vulnerable, and we don't like being exposed in certain ways. Maybe we aren't seeing the results we were hoping for yet and it seems futile to continue. Or maybe doing what's right calls us too far out of our comfort zone. Following God's plan isn't always easy to do, and it requires a measure of faith to walk out.

But, friend, sticking with the right thing and watching God work through you will create a level of joy nothing else can touch. It will bring healing to your weary soul. There is something wonderful about a job well done, especially knowing it has eternal rewards. And in those moments where discouragement tries to set in, God will be there, ready to bring encouragement, strength, wisdom, and compassion to reignite your desire for the work He has created specifically for you. And in the end, you will receive a blessing from God that will make all the hard work well worth your time and effort.

Dear God, thank You for using me to bless others and further Your kingdom. Let me not grow weary as I do! Amen.

CAREFUL PLANNING MATTERS

Careful planning puts you ahead in the long run;
hurry and scurry puts you further behind.
PROVERBS 21:5 MSG

Protecting our calendars is important so we can be intentional about how we spend our time. This is a huge challenge for us women, especially when trying to manage the busyness of a family. Arranging our schedules in God-honoring ways takes careful planning. When we do, we will be blessed for our diligence.

What does your calendar look like? Is each day so full that tasks get left undone? Is an overabundance of appointments and meetings taking up family time? Are there any breaks in the action? Do you continually feel behind because you are unable to meet all the demands? Friend, be kind to yourself and mindful of God's desires. His plan never included going ninety miles an hour, seven days a week. And if your schedule looks like that, set it before the Lord and ask for His wisdom. Let Him show you how to plan with purpose so you have the strength and energy to care for yourself, the ability to bless your family with peace, and time to spend with God on a regular basis.

Dear God, show me how to slow down so I have margin to do what matters the most. Amen.

IN THE MORNING

Let me see your kindness to me in the morning, for I am trusting you. Show me where to walk, for my prayer is sincere.

PSALM 143:8 TLB

Let prayer be on your lips before your feet hit the floor. Start the day with soul-soothing prayer that helps set you in the right direction. Even if you're struggling, talking to God first thing will bring a balance to the morning that will carry throughout the day. It's the best thing you can do for your heart—be it anxious or not.

We need the Lord to guide us. We need Him to show us the way. It's not that we're incapable women. We are strong and wise, no doubt. But it's that He sees the whole picture. God understands the complexity of what the day will hold. And trusting Him from sunup to sundown gives us an anchor to cling to when unexpected storms hit. Holding fast to God brings balance and buoyancy, keeping our heads above the choppy waters. Start the day with prayer and expect to see God's blessings.

Dear God, show me kindness in the morning as I press into You for strength to navigate the storms the day may bring. Let me be anchored in Your goodness so I can withstand them all. Amen.

A STEADFAST MIND

"You will keep in perfect and constant peace the one whose mind is steadfast [that is, committed and focused on You—in both inclination and character], because he trusts and takes refuge in You [with hope and confident expectation]."

ISAIAH 26:3 AMP

When you're feeling destabilized by life's challenges, turn your mind to Jesus. Stop what you're doing and think about the goodness of God you've seen manifested in your life. Rather than focusing on your circumstances, remember the times God showed up. Rest as you think through moments when you felt His compassion. Pause for a bit to recall the peace you felt that made no sense based on the situation at hand. Keep your mind steadfast on the ways God wrapped you up and brought comfort. And then choose to take refuge in God once again.

Life is going to punch you in the gut. There's no way to escape hardship and pain. Your time on planet Earth will never be fair or easy—at least not for long. But through it all, you can have hope and confidence. You can be expectant for God to nourish your weary soul. You can trust Him to show up.

Dear God, help me trust You no matter what, so I can experience perfect and constant peace, knowing You're working out situations on my behalf. Amen.

GOD'S PLAN WILL STAND

Many plans are in a man's mind, but it is the LORD's purpose for him that will stand (be carried out).

PROVERBS 19:21 AMP

Friend, maybe it's time for you to rest in the truth that God's plan for your life will work out. Aren't you tired of playing God, trying to manipulate the outcome? Have you been working the angles, hoping to control situations? We often think we know what we need, and so we try to make it happen. Rather than rest in God's sovereignty, we meddle in each moment. We take the wheel. We end up exasperated and exhausted. And we lose hope.

But take heart! Scripture reminds us that we can let go and let God. We don't have to have everything figured out. Our plans aren't set in stone and unchangeable in His hands. The Lord will always have the last word when it comes to our walking out our purpose. We just need to trust Him. And as we take steps forward, we can do so with hearts of expectation. We can plan, knowing that God has our backs and will intervene if needed. So take in a deep breath of His goodness and exhale as you rest. God's got you.

Dear God, help me cease striving and trust that Your plan for my life will stand. Amen.

STORING UP IN HEAVEN

"Sell what you have and give to those in need. This will fatten your purses in heaven! And the purses of heaven have no rips or holes in them. Your treasures there will never disappear; no thief can steal them; no moth can destroy them. Wherever your treasure is, there your heart and thoughts will also be."

LUKE 12:33–34 TLB

Care for yourself enough to store up eternal treasures in heaven. This requires you to be mindful of your spiritual health so you'll know how to walk out the storing up of heavenly treasures in the day-to-day. Unless you connect with the Father and understand His heart for the lost and broken, doing so will be impossible. But when your soul is nourished daily by God, you'll long to store up those treasures.

Ask the Lord to open your eyes and ears to see and hear His leading. Reject the world's pull to collect earthly trinkets, for they have no heavenly value. Invest in people and relationships, pouring into them your time and treasure. Keep an eternal perspective so you're not swayed by fleeting emotions. And be a light-bearer, shining God's goodness into a parched land. Let your words and actions be focused on eternity.

Dear God, my heart is with You, so let my life reflect that allegiance every day and in every way. Amen.

WHAT ROLE ARE YOU TO PLAY?

But Moses said to the people, "Don't be afraid. Stand your ground, and watch the Lord *rescue you today. The Egyptians you see today you will never ever see again. The* Lord *will fight for you. You just keep still."*

Exodus 14:13–14 CEB

In a world where we're always busy fighting battles and trying to calm the waters ourselves, today's scripture passage is a treasure. There's a time for us to pick up the sword and fight and a time to watch as God does. How do you know which time it is? Ask God.

Regardless, there's no reason to be afraid. God sees you right where you are. He has already gone before you and made provision. The Lord will give you strength to stand your ground, whether it's to watch Him rescue or for you to engage. He will give the emotional, physical, and spiritual health to take the next step. So, friend, stay close to God and talk to Him about every challenge, asking for guidance on the role you're to play. He knows what's best. And you can rest in Him with confidence and courage.

Dear God, help me seek You when the battles come so I know if I'm to engage or watch You do so. Help me trust that You have me in the palm of Your mighty and capable hand. Amen.

AT THE END OF OURSELVES

God, listen to my cry; pay attention to my prayer! When my heart is weak, I cry out to you from the very ends of the earth. Lead me to the rock that is higher than I am because you have been my refuge, a tower of strength in the face of the enemy.

Psalm 61:1–3 CEB

Sometimes life feels too big to navigate. In our stubbornness, we often try to figure things out. We don't reach out to our support groups of friends and family. We don't call a counselor, pastor, or small group leader. We don't seek out resources. Eventually, we hit rock bottom. Our hearts feel weak. And that's when we cry out to God.

Letting ourselves get to that place of emotional depletion isn't healthy, especially because the Lord promises to be our refuge. He will be our strong tower. And when we rest in His goodness and trust in His faithfulness, we'll find that our needs are met in supernatural ways. He will saturate us in His love, strengthening us to continue.

Dear God, I confess the times I try to navigate the ups and downs of life alone. Forgive me for doubting Your compassion and willingness to help. In those moments, remind me that You are always there for me. Amen.

NOTHING OF THIS WORLD

Charm and grace are deceptive, and [superficial] beauty is vain,
but a woman who fears the Lord *[reverently worshiping, obeying,*
serving, and trusting Him with awe-filled respect], she shall be praised.
Proverbs 31:30 AMP

Sometimes we put all our effort into bettering ourselves the world's ways. We focus on getting lean and strong bodies to stay attractive. We spend thousands on supplements and products that promise to maintain our youth. We purchase the latest trends in clothing to look up-to-date. And we go under the knife in hopes of altering our bodies so they meet society's standards of beauty. In the end, we lose our joy because nothing of this world can satisfy the longing in our hearts.

But God can. As a matter of fact, He is our only hope for sustained joy and a fullness in our hearts. The Lord will bring life to our dry bones, withered by the stressors of life. He will restore our weary souls. So choose today to invest your time in loving God and see how it changes things for the better.

Dear God, I've spent too much time trying to find validation from the world. My self-care has been motivated by earthly acceptance. Forgive me. Moving forward, help me to invest my time in deepening my relationship with You. Amen.

WHEN STUBBORNNESS IS GOOD

And the Lord replied, "I myself will go with you and give you success." For Moses had said, "If you aren't going with us, don't let us move a step from this place."

EXODUS 33:14–15 TLB

Above all else, trust in God to direct your next steps. You don't have to figure everything out yourself. Your successes are not up to you alone. Instead, recognize the power of God's presence in your circumstances. And if you're stubborn at all, let it be a refusal to take the next step without His leading.

God is faithful and trustworthy in every way. If you ask, He will guide you on the path determined long before your entrance onto the kingdom calendar. You will be able to rest in the Lord in all things as He reignites the light inside you. So let Him be what steadies you in this chaotic world. Let Him bring a balance to your anxious heart through His comfort and compassion. Cling to Him for joy and wisdom, knowing there is no substitute for His presence in your life. And when you surrender to Him in such ways, you're making a deliberate decision to be kind to yourself that will bring forth beautiful blessings!

Dear God, help me to be determined to wait for Your leading. Help me to be persistent as I cling to You for guidance. Allow me to find joy and comfort in Your presence today. Amen.

GOD VALUES REST

It is senseless for you to work so hard from early morning until late at night, fearing you will starve to death; for God wants his loved ones to get their proper rest.

PSALM 127:2 TLB

What does your schedule look like right now? Are you running from appointment to meeting to responsibility? Is your day packed from the moment your feet hit the floor till your eyes close at the day's end? Do you feel pressure to do more just to keep up? Friend, this isn't how God wants your calendar to look. His plan isn't for you to be exhausted and depleted each night. Quite the opposite, in fact.

Consider that God values rest. He knows the demands on our lives and sees the pressure we face to do more and be more. He understands our panicky feelings as we struggle to meet our basic needs. But instead of sitting in that exhaustion or pushing harder, we're to trust in God's provision. We're to rest in His presence, knowing our strength will be restored and our souls will be nourished in supernatural ways.

Dear God, I'm tired and overwhelmed in my own strength. Forgive me for subscribing to the world's solutions regarding my schedule. Instead, let me remember that You are my source and I can rest in You every day. Amen.

BE READY

"Everyone would be ready for him if they knew the exact hour of his return—just as they would be ready for a thief if they knew when he was coming. So be ready all the time. For I, the Messiah, will come when least expected."

LUKE 12:39–40 TLB

Scripture tells us that Jesus will return in an instant. We may not know the time and date, but we can be confident that He will come back for all believers at the perfect moment. Until then we're to be ready. Are you?

You may wonder how to prepare for the rapture. Along with being a true believer—recognizing Jesus as God's only Son whose death on the cross paid your sin debt once and for all and who then rose again three days later—you need to be investing in your spiritual health. You can do this by spending time in God's Word daily, digging deeper into what God says through scripture and meditating on His promises. You can talk to God continually through prayer. You can live in obedience, taking the Lord's commands seriously. And you can let your light shine into the world so others have the opportunity to meet the Lord and secure their own salvation.

Dear God, I am ready for Your return and excited to be with You forever. Come, Lord Jesus! Amen.

A BED OF PEACE

Tonight I will sleep securely on a bed of peace because I trust You, You alone, O Eternal One, will keep me safe.

PSALM 4:8 VOICE

Today's verse offers beautiful imagery of what resting in the Lord looks like. It tells us we'll find sleep on a bed of peace because of our decision to trust. Friend, where are you choosing to trust God today? Is your marriage on the rocks and you're praying for a miracle? Has a child departed from the faith and you are believing God will restore them soon? Are the bills bigger than the money coming in each month, leaving you to trust in God's provision? Did the doctor deliver discouraging news and you're choosing to stand in expectation for healing? Remain in that posture until peace overflows you.

It's hard to rest in the Lord because we're women of action. And when we're feeling scared and desperate, we want to see immediate change. But as we wait for God to act, we can experience divine peace that will settle and soothe our souls in powerful ways. And to get there, we need to trust God to be God.

Dear God, I believe You will show up, but please help my unbelief when I struggle in the waiting. You are a good, good Father and won't ever turn Your back on me. Bless me today with peace as I trust You. Amen.

REST IN THE LORD

Rest in the Lord; wait patiently for him to act.
Don't be envious of evil men who prosper.
PSALM 37:7 TLB

Waiting for God to show up can be hard, especially when we see others enjoying life. We live in a microwave society where we want what we want—now. Too often we strive in our own strength because we're anxious to move things along. We push ourselves to work hard to get what we want. And our days become a blur as we whiz through them, going from one thing to the next in desperation. Sound familiar?

What would it look like for you to rest in the Lord? Maybe it's stepping back from the busyness and spending time in God's Word instead. Maybe it's giving up control over those stressful circumstances. Maybe it's choosing not to orchestrate every detail, releasing the desire to manipulate the outcome. Maybe it's remembering His perfect track record in your life, realizing you're safe in His capable hands. Maybe it's asking Him to help you rest and wait. Whatever it may be, being women of faith means we trust God to show up and meet our needs in ways that make a difference. And doing so brings peace and joy in abundance.

Dear God, give me patience to wait and faith to trust. I know You will always show up! Amen.

STEPPING OUT OF THE TRAFFIC

"Step out of the traffic! Take a long, loving look at me, your High God, above politics, above everything."
PSALM 46:10 MSG

There are times when the best thing we can do for our mental and emotional health is press PAUSE. Taking a break from the craziness of our schedules does wonders for our minds because it provides moments of clarity. It gives us a chance to seek God and listen for His still, small voice in fresh ways. And stepping out of the traffic of our days allows a new perspective to shine forth, bringing refreshment to our overwhelmed hearts.

There will never be a shortage of "traffic" in life. Be it in our marriage, our jobs, our parenting, our friendships, or our own personal challenges, we'll eventually find ourselves bumper to bumper, crowded by responsibilities pressing in on all sides. Friend, that's why it's so important to keep our eyes fixed on God first and foremost. Our heart needs to stay trained on Him and His Word. And if we ask, He will lovingly navigate us through this life in peace and recharge us for the journey.

Dear God, somehow my life got crazy busy and I'm struggling to keep up with it all. It leaves me feeling overwhelmed and frustrated, and that's not Your plan for me. Help me press PAUSE and regroup with You in the driver's seat. Amen.

GOD'S PROTECTION AND PROVISION

Your mind will be clear, free from fear; when you lie down to rest, you will be refreshed by sweet sleep. Stay calm; there is no need to be afraid of a sudden disaster or to worry when calamity strikes the wicked, for the Eternal is always there to protect you. He will safeguard your each and every step.

PROVERBS 3:24–26 VOICE

How would you go about each day differently if you believed God would protect you? If you had faith that each step forward was fortified, would you have more courage to step out of your comfort zone? Sometimes we get stuck in our head, worried about circumstances that may or may not come to pass, and it robs us of joy and depletes us of peace.

Talk to God about those worries and fears. You can be honest with Him because He understands your feelings even better than you do. Invite the Lord into those vulnerable moments when you're struggling to calm your anxious heart, and let Him care for you. Trust God to give you rest and hope. And watch as He replenishes you to step out again, trusting in His protection and provision.

Dear God, in those times when I can't care for myself, will You care for me? I want to be free from fear and worry because they weigh me down, but I need courage and comfort that come from Your hand. Amen.

LETTING GOD SATISFY

I will satisfy those who are weary, and I will refresh every soul in the grips of sorrow.
JEREMIAH 31:25 VOICE

The world offers all sorts of solutions to revive a weary or sorrowful heart, but are they right for us? We could engage in retail therapy, spending money we may not have. We could partake in libations or substances that promise to numb the pain, if only for a while. We could get lost in a salacious novel that leads us into temptation. We could mindlessly binge crass movies on a streaming service. Or we could surf the web and potentially find ourselves tangled in the wrong things. All of these are available at any time, but they are misleading and short-lived.

On the other hand, God promises to comfort us in healthy and loving ways that are good for us and glorify Him. It costs us nothing but faith. It requires nothing from us but asking and receiving. And it deepens our relationships with the Lord. Does your soul need refreshment and restoration? Are you drained and disillusioned? Forget the world, for it has no lasting solution. Instead, go right to God and find the nourishment you need.

Dear God, thank You for being the answer to everything I need. Thank You for understanding the feelings that bog me down. Refresh my soul today. Amen.

OUR NEED FOR NOURISHMENT

We live within the shadow of the Almighty, sheltered by the God who is above all gods. This I declare, that he alone is my refuge, my place of safety; he is my God, and I am trusting him.

PSALM 91:1–2 TLB

Today's scripture reminds us of who God is to those who love Him. It's a good reminder because sometimes we forget about the Lord's magnificence. We forget He is our place of safety where we can find rest. We overlook that He's our refuge, promising protection from danger and trouble. We don't remember we live within His shadow, signifying His magnitude in relation to our own. And God shields us, offering shelter to those of faith. This is why we can trust the Lord to help us find balance again when our world is shaken.

What a privilege to serve a God who understands our need for nourishment. He sees the joy-draining circumstances that suck us dry. He knows the situations that threaten to dim the light within all believers. And in Him we can enjoy respite and relaxation for our souls.

Dear God, I confess that I sometimes forget who You are. I get stuck in managing my mess and forget that You are all-knowing, all-powerful, and ever present. Forgive me for forgetting Your awesomeness, and thank You for nursing me back to emotional and spiritual health when I need it. Amen.

STANDING SILENTLY BEFORE THE LORD

I stand silently before the Lord, waiting for him to rescue me. For salvation comes from him alone. Yes, he alone is my Rock, my rescuer, defense and fortress. Why then should I be tense with fear when troubles come?

PSALM 62:1–2 TLB

Stress and tension do nothing to help us out. Being full of worry and angst only works against us. When we let fear rule the day, we're left struggling to find joy and peace. And many of us flail under the pressure of it all, desperate to find balance in mind and heart once again.

Faith comes into play when we realize we're at the end of ourselves, when we're out of options, hitting the limits of our humanity. We stand silently before the Lord and wait for help. We recognize our frailty and inability to rescue and restore. And we fall into His arms, finding rest and reassurance. At times we cry out for God's help, but at other times no words are needed. In His sovereignty, He is fully aware of our depleted places and will bring encouragement to our souls.

Dear God, thank You for seeing me and the challenges I'm facing. Thank You for understanding them all without me even saying a word. With You is the only place I want to be. Amen.

WHEN WE'RE BROKEN

I admit how broken I am in body and spirit,
but God is my strength, and He will be mine forever.
PSALM 73:26 VOICE

Life has a special way of breaking us into pieces, both in body and in spirit. We may have navigated a difficult marriage for years only to have it end in divorce. We may have lost children to the pressures of the world, unable to save them from the hurt. Maybe we couldn't keep up with incoming bills, and filing bankruptcy was the only option. Maybe a longtime friend betrayed our confidence, and the heartbreak feels like too much. Or maybe the medical treatment didn't work as hoped, and we lost someone very special. Life is hard.

When we feel broken, God is our only strength. He is the one who can bring us back to health and wholeness. We may look to the world for solutions. We may expect friends and family to fix us. But they'll fall short because it's not their job or skill set. Admit to God how broken you are, and watch as He puts you back together so you'll shine once again.

Dear God, I come to You in pieces today, asking to be restored by Your capable hands. You know every detail, and You see the path forward. Please help me find wholeness again. Amen.

NOTHING IS IMPOSSIBLE

"For with God nothing [is or ever] shall be impossible."
LUKE 1:37 AMP

Today's verse tells us that when we press into God for help, all things are possible. But let's remember that what we're asking for may not be His will. His answer might look completely different than what we hoped for—what we prayed for. But let this be a reminder that with the Lord, absolutely nothing is impossible. He can do all things! And if it's His will, it will come to pass without fail.

That means we can take a step back and catch our breath. We can stop pushing so hard, trying to make things happen our way and on our timeline. We can sleep without worry and rest without stress. We don't have to carry the burden of making ends meet, for God is the one in control. And rather than try to manipulate circumstances, we can go to the Lord and trust His will to prevail. It may be easier said than done, but let it be a blessing! Think about it: Where do you need to walk this out in your life?

Dear God, help me understand that just because everything is possible with You, it doesn't mean everything I want is good and right. Help me breathe and rest, knowing Your will for me is best! Amen.

DELIGHTING IN THE LORD

Revel in his holy Name, God-seekers, be jubilant! Study God and his strength, seek his presence day and night; remember all the wonders he performed, the miracles and judgments that came out of his mouth.

1 Chronicles 16:10–12 MSG

The very best thing we can do for ourselves is delight in the Lord because it takes our minds off our struggles and puts them on His strength. It encourages us to seek His presence over our problems. We focus on His goodness over our glitches. We bask in God's trustworthiness rather than our tribulations. And it's good for our emotional health.

Spend time today thinking about the ways God has shown up for you. Do you keep a journal of them? Let yourself revisit seasons when He got you out of a tight spot. Remember the moments when peace washed over you, calming your anxious heart. Meditate on the Lord's wisdom through the opened and closed doors you've experienced in life. Ask Him to bring to mind unexplainable joy that burst forth in the midst of hardship as well as the comfort that engulfed you in the middle of chaotic circumstances. Reminisce about God's kindness and generosity throughout the years and how He has blessed you in unexpected ways. These memories help revive a weary soul by reminding you of God's great compassion. And sometimes we need to rejoice in His holy name to reset our hearts and minds.

Dear God, I delight in You! Amen.

GOD JOYFULLY CELEBRATES OVER YOU

The Eternal your God is standing right here among you,
and He is the champion who will rescue you. He will joyfully
celebrate over you; He will rest in His love for you;
He will joyfully sing because of you like a new husband.
ZEPHANIAH 3:17 VOICE

Do you know that God joyfully celebrates over you? Sometimes we think we must have it all together to be loved. We feel inadequate, like we don't measure up to His standards of righteousness. We obsess over our imperfections and shortcomings. And we doubt our goodness. But God loves us and accepts us just as we are—right now, in this moment.

It's time to be kind to ourselves and ask God to silence our harsh inner critic. You know, the voice that whispers hurtful things day in and day out. If the Lord doesn't expect flawlessness, why do we? If He's full of grace for us, why can't we extend it to ourselves? If God forgives our failings, why can't we do the same? Let Him teach you to rest in His love and compassion so you can learn to see yourself as He does.

Dear God, it does my heart good to know You joyfully celebrate over me. I love that I bring You delight, even though it's hard to reconcile at times. Help me see myself through Your eyes. Amen.

TRUSTING GIVES STRENGTH

But those who trust in the Eternal One will regain their strength.
They will soar on wings as eagles. They will run—never winded,
never weary. They will walk—never tired, never faint.
Isaiah 40:31 VOICE

Trusting God will strengthen you for the battles life brings your way. Giving up control and putting faith in a God you cannot see may seem counterintuitive, but doing so will yield powerful results. You will feel lighter inside, like a weight has been lifted. You will have stamina and endurance for the journey ahead. And you will be able to find courage to take the next step forward, clinging to God for guidance through it.

In contrast, every time we hoard control as we try to fix things on our own, we only increase our anxiety and stress. It knocks us off-balance, which feels destabilizing. We're not meant to fly solo. We need God's direction, which sometimes comes through godly friends and family and the wisdom they provide. So when we trust God, we're making a deliberate choice to pray, dig into the Word, and surround ourselves with people who point us to Him. And when we do, weariness won't weigh us down.

Dear God, help me choose to trust You over taking on my battles alone. Unless I trust You, I'll continue to feel tired and overwhelmed and weak. I need You to help me get through each day. Amen.

HOLY AND WHOLE

May God himself, the God who makes everything holy and whole, make you holy and whole, put you together—spirit, soul, and body—and keep you fit for the coming of our Master, Jesus Christ. The One who called you is completely dependable. If he said it, he'll do it!

1 THESSALONIANS 5:23–24 MSG

It's no wonder we struggle to feel holy and whole in a world that pulls us in a million different directions. Sometimes it feels almost impossible to stand strong when our heart is splintered. We worry about a child who is struggling to find a place in the world. We have anxiety about trusting in a new marriage or rejuvenating an existing one. We're fearful that our income won't be able to keep up with monthly bills. We feel disconnected because some of our key friendships have been strained. And rather than feel all put together, we struggle to feel healed and healthy.

But, friend, God promises to restore us when we are broken. And if we will let Him, He will be the glue that holds us securely together the next time a fracture threatens. The Lord will nourish and mend us because He is dependable.

Dear God, put me back together again and hold me tight so I can be holy and whole through Your kind and generous hand. Amen.

THE POWER OF SCRIPTURE

By your words I can see where I'm going; they throw a beam of light on my dark path. I've committed myself and I'll never turn back from living by your righteous order.

PSALM 119:105–106 MSG

What a blessing to know that through God's Word we will find our next steps. He's ready and willing to shine His light through scripture, showing the path we're to follow. So, when we're unclear about what choices to make, the best thing we can do is meditate on God's Word. He will give clarity so we can walk in ways that are true and right. And that is what will bring joy back into our lives.

When we're out of sync with God's will, the Holy Spirit will nudge us. We'll feel it deep in our souls. It may manifest as an unsettling feeling in our guts or fogginess in our minds, but we'll know something is off. And because of God's great love and compassion, He will convict us in hopes that we will seek His path forward through time spent in His Word. Without fail, His Word will give us guidance and comfort.

Dear God, thank You for the Bible and the power it brings into my life. Help me open it every day, sitting with scripture to find help and hope to navigate this crazy life. Amen.

IMMERSED IN THE TRUTH

Immerse them in the truth, the truth Your voice speaks.
In the same way You sent Me into this world, I am sending them.
JOHN 17:17–18 VOICE

What a beautiful prayer from Jesus to the Father. He is asking God to saturate us in truth so we'll know how to live this life in healthy ways—emotionally, physically, and spiritually. Rather than depend on the world to educate us—knowing their ways will be self-seeking and evil at the core—He wants truth to prevail. Jesus wants truth to bring balance and harmony to our souls with pure nourishment our culture cannot replicate. And we'll need that truth to be coursing through our hearts and minds as we fulfill the call to spread the gospel to those around us.

There is only one way your little light will be able to shine forth, and it's through faith in the Lord. The more we invest in that relationship, the brighter it shines. The more we embrace God's goodness and pass it along, the bigger the flame in us becomes. And with it comes uncontainable joy and peace that others can't explain in earthly terms. So, yes, Lord, immerse us in the truth today and always! Strengthen our resolve to live in ways that point others to You.

Dear God, thank You for loving me with such immeasurable depth. Amen.

RICHLY INHABIT

Let the word of the Anointed One richly inhabit your lives. With all wisdom teach, counsel, and instruct one another. Sing the psalms, compose hymns and songs inspired by the Spirit, and keep on singing—sing to God from hearts full and spilling over with thankfulness.

COLOSSIANS 3:16 VOICE

When we don't dig into the Word daily, we're spiritually starving ourselves. Without encouragement from a community of believers, our souls will be parched. And without releasing joyful praise from within, our spirits will wither. It takes intentionality to bring nourishment that heals and restores. God may be the giver, but we must pursue Him with purpose and passion. Just like earthly relationships, being in a healthy relationship with God requires give and take. It requires effort. And as God begins to richly inhabit your life through time spent together, it will strengthen you, body and soul. Joy will spill forth, and your life will begin to reflect His goodness, helping others see the need for the Lord in their own lives.

Where do you need to make changes in your walk with God? What part of your spiritual health are you ignoring? Where is the Holy Spirit calling you to wade into deeper waters? Where is your soul crying out to be richly inhabited?

Dear God, I crave a richer relationship with You. Help me to seek You daily! Amen.

FINDING THE PERFECT BALANCE

The Voice took on flesh and became human and chose to live alongside us. We have seen Him, enveloped in undeniable splendor—the one true Son of the Father—evidenced in the perfect balance of grace and truth.

JOHN 1:14 VOICE

If the Lord can find the perfect balance between grace and truth, He can help you find the perfect balance in your life too. Maybe you're working too many hours or working inefficiently and are constantly exhausted. Maybe you've been unable to block your day wisely so there's enough time to meet the needs of those who matter the most. Maybe you're being too grace-filled rather than holding others accountable. Maybe you're giving too much to others and not taking time to nurture yourself. Or maybe you're too self-focused at the expense of those you love. Balance is important.

We may not be able to find the perfect balance ourselves, but when we invite God into our daily schedules and let Him prioritize, that's a healthy start. His plan isn't for us to run at a breakneck pace and end each day running on fumes. Hard work is good and necessary, but God will help us navigate our calendars so they benefit us and glorify Him.

Dear God, I'm tired of being tired. Help me follow Your will for each day. Amen.

TRUE AND LASTING NOURISHMENT

The Spirit brings life. The flesh has nothing to offer. The words I have been teaching you are spirit and life, but some of you do not believe. From the first day Jesus began to call disciples, He knew those who did not have genuine faith. He knew, too, who would betray Him.

JOHN 6:63–64 VOICE

It's the Spirit who ushers in true and lasting nourishment, not our flesh. The world may offer tempting possibilities that look promising, but they don't deliver. They're short-lived and underwhelming. Be it retail therapy, comfort foods, numbing substances, salacious novels or movies, or the temptation to hide away from community, the euphoric results such things provide are fleeting. And in the end, our souls are left hungry and parched. In our efforts to be kind to ourselves, we did the exact opposite.

Unless one has a genuine faith in Jesus, this kind of nourishment is all they know. But as believers, we know it's the Holy Spirit in us who brings generous refreshment. He's a game changer because He's exactly what we need to foster and support our health—emotionally, physically, and spiritually. The Spirit will use our time in God's Word and in prayer to make us wholehearted again.

Dear God, forgive me for looking to anyone or anything else to bring nourishment to my hungry soul. Let it always be You alone. Amen.

HUMBLY GLAD FOR THE MESSAGE

So get rid of all that is wrong in your life, both inside and outside, and humbly be glad for the wonderful message we have received, for it is able to save our souls as it takes hold of our hearts.

JAMES 1:21 TLB

Friend, grab on to God's Word and never let it go, because it is life-changing in every way. It will convict you of what thoughts and habits need to go. It will convince you to trust God—not yourself—to be God. It will create space to let the Lord speak truth into your life. It will cause a shift in your heart, and you will want to pursue righteous living above worldly living. It will cultivate salvation as you let the Holy Spirit regenerate your heart. God's Word will never let you down. It saves and restores. And even more, it will never lose its power to bring transformation when you dig into scripture.

What message has God been speaking to you lately? What bad thoughts or behaviors do you need to get rid of? What verses are connecting with your spirit in new and fresh ways? Friend, let the Lord bring health to you, body, soul, and mind. Let His Word sink deep into your DNA and bring hope and healing where and when you need it.

Dear God, Your words are powerful tools in my life. Let me seek them out daily, humbly accepting their life-changing messages. Amen.

JOY VERSUS HAPPINESS

You will show me the path of life; in Your presence is fullness of joy; in Your right hand there are pleasures forevermore.

PSALM 16:11 AMP

If you're lacking joy because life has beaten you down, then today's scripture should be a real encouragement to you! Sometimes we think finding joy is up to us, so we try to bring it forward with earthly goodies. We equate joy with happiness and work for temporal things with fervor. Maybe we go on a diet or try to start new, healthier habits. Maybe we join a group of people with the same interests or pursuits. Maybe we set fresh routines in our day for better time management or look for new work opportunities. Or maybe we cultivate new relationships, hoping they will fill empty places inside.

But when we do these things, we're forgetting there's a big difference between happiness and joy. Consider that your happiness is dependent on earthly circumstances. Joy, on the other hand, can be a constant blessing we experience as believers, even if life is chaotic. Why? Because joy is a fruit of the Spirit that comes from living in God's presence alone. And He promises to bless us with abundant joy as we spend time with Him.

Dear God, let me stay close to You in the highs and lows of life, because in Your presence is where true joy is possible. Amen.

CHOOSING TO OBEY

"If you keep My commandments and obey My teaching, you will remain in My love, just as I have kept My Father's commandments and remain in His love. I have told you these things so that My joy and delight may be in you, and that your joy may be made full and complete and overflowing."

JOHN 15:10–11 AMP

Obedience is a constant message in God's Word, but too often we rebel against it. Why? Because we don't always like being told what to do. Can we just be honest? As adults, we often feel certain we know what's best. And since we're educated and have a wide range of life experiences to pull from, we decide we're in the know. But that mindset tells God we can manage life without Him. Even though He's our Creator and fully aware of us down to the last detail, we think ourselves smarter.

But consider that our obedience shows God that we love Him. It's an act of worship as we recognize our position in regard to His. And choosing to follow the Lord's will and ways creates joy in us—joy that is complete and overflowing. Letting God lead is a healthy self-care decision because it blesses us through and through.

Dear God, help me delight in keeping Your commands every day and in every way. Amen.

THE GREAT PHYSICIAN

O Lord my God, I pleaded with you, and you gave me my health again. You brought me back from the brink of the grave, from death itself, and here I am alive!

PSALM 30:2–3 TLB

When your health is failing—be it emotional, physical, or spiritual—cry out to God. He can bring you back from where you are in that moment. He can help you understand your feelings with better clarity so you can get out of your head. He can heal your illness or condition. And through His Spirit living in you, God can call you into deeper waters of faith to restore a weary soul. The Lord knows where your health is thriving and diving, and as the Great Physician, He is fully capable of meeting any deficit you're experiencing. Have you asked for His help?

Take time today to pray with complete honesty. Of course, God already knows all about you and your needs, but go ahead and pour your heart out to your Father. Tell Him every fear and worry. Tell Him where you're hurting and hopeless. Talk to the Lord about the feelings that are weighing you down. And then watch as He brings comfort or healing or wisdom or endurance in His great love.

Dear God, I trust You to give me my health again! Amen.

GIVING PATIENCE A CHANCE

Dear brothers, is your life full of difficulties and temptations? Then be happy, for when the way is rough, your patience has a chance to grow. So let it grow, and don't try to squirm out of your problems. For when your patience is finally in full bloom, then you will be ready for anything, strong in character, full and complete.

JAMES 1:2–4 TLB

James 1:2–4 provides a prescription for resting in the Lord. Unless we follow it, we won't have the strength to stay the course and let ourselves be molded by life experiences. God may have allowed them but only because His plan is to use each difficulty and temptation for our good and His glory. That means that each time we feel overwhelmed by our situations, we need to rest in Him. When we do, we will give patience a chance to grow into a mighty tool.

Too often we try to hide from problems. We let our goal be to fly under the radar. And rather than deal with each struggle, we want to ignore or self-medicate. But, friend, those aren't healthy responses. Why hide under your covers when you can hide in the Lord? Rest in God and let Him navigate you through each step with courage and confidence. Wait and follow His leading. Then you'll be ready for anything.

Dear God, teach me to stay the course rather than run from struggles. Amen.

TURNING SORROWS INTO JOY

"Hear me, Lord; oh, have pity and help me."
Then he turned my sorrow into joy! He took away my clothes of mourning and clothed me with joy.
PSALM 30:10–11 TLB

God understands our innermost feelings. He knows when they are spot-on and when they're completely off base. He understands our flare for drama at times. God sees those painful moments that knock us to our knees, leaving us scared and hopeless. He knows the depth of our grief when we lose someone special or something important. The Lord has full knowledge of our parenting fears that rob us of peace. He's aware of our marriage struggles that break our hearts. He sees the disappointments others don't even recognize. And God even understands the complexities within us that we don't understand. That's why, when we ask God for help, He will bring balance and restoration.

Rather than stewing in your feelings, have you prayed about what's bothering you? Have you sat in God's Word, letting scripture bring refreshment to your soul? Have you meditated on key verses in expectation of hearing God's voice? Seek the Lord and let Him bring comfort by turning sorrows into joy!

Dear God, thank You for knowing me completely and understanding my feelings even when I don't. Please heal my heart and clothe me with joy! Amen.

YOU CAN'T SAVE YOURSELF

I will praise You because You answered me when I was in trouble. You have become my salvation.

PSALM 118:21 VOICE

To whom do you look to be saved? When life gets too big and circumstances feel too heavy, where do you look for deliverance? We may phone a friend or cry with a family member, but most of us try to figure out our problems alone. We do that because we are embarrassed or worried about what others might think. Or we might have a pride issue and not want to look weak or incapable. Or it could be because we've always had to fix things ourselves. But the reality is that God alone is our salvation. He is all we need.

Let Him rekindle that spark in you. It may be dim right now, but the Lord can reignite that light effortlessly. Press in and watch as He brings relief from trouble, offering a new perspective and hope. There's no reason to alienate yourself when hard times hit. As self-sufficient as you are, friend, you can't save yourself. It's not your job. Instead, pray for rescue, and then praise God for His reliability.

Dear God, I need You to help me. I'm tired of trying to fix life by myself. I know You're my salvation, and I'm looking to You for deliverance so I can shine brightly once again for Your kingdom. Amen.

RECOUNTING THE WAYS

My mouth will repeat your righteous acts and your saving deeds all day long. I don't even know how many of those there are! I will dwell on your mighty acts, my Lord. Lord, I will help others remember nothing but your righteous deeds.

Psalm 71:15–16 CEB

Pure joy overflows when we think about the times and ways God has saved us. Recounting His goodness encourages a weary soul. We need those reminders, especially when we're struggling. We need to remember that God has been there for us before, because it gives confidence that He will be again.

Today, bring those God moments to mind. Sit with them and give Him the glory. Did the Lord bring physical or emotional healing? Did He provide a godly community of believers when you felt alone? Did He open doors for work or financial relief? Was your marriage healed in unexpected ways? Has your wayward child returned to the right path in life? Have fear and worry lost their grip, being replaced by an unexplainable peace? Are you navigating tricky relationships with a renewed sense of grace? Let joy over these times reign in your heart!

Dear God, You have been so faithful to me. Your track record is perfect, and that brings unshakable faith that You will show up again. Amen.

REJECTED BY THE WORLD

If you find that the world despises you, remember that before it despised you, it first despised Me. If you were a product of the world order, then it would love you. But you are not a product of the world because I have taken you out of it, and it despises you for that very reason.

JOHN 15:18–19 VOICE

Be kind to yourself, friend. Lower your expectations of worldly acceptance. Release your hope of being loved and adored by this culture. Stop trying to fit into earthly standards of beauty. Let go of your desire to keep up with others who busy themselves by collecting treasures here. Quit working harder and longer to make a name for yourself. This is not your home, and the world is not your source of value.

Instead, build your faith in God. Invest in a thriving relationship with Him. And be ready to experience rejection as you stop striving for the adoration and approval of the world. When we're called to salvation, even though we're still here, we're taken out of this culture. It's no longer what drives us because we're new creations with an eternal perspective. And becoming a believer is how we find balance and restoration for our souls. It's how we live with joy. And it's how we shine Jesus into this dark world.

Dear God, my heart and home are with You. Amen.

TEMPTED BUT NOT SINFUL

Happy is the man who doesn't give in and do wrong when he is tempted, for afterwards he will get as his reward the crown of life that God has promised those who love him.

JAMES 1:12 TLB

We will face temptations of all kinds in our lifetime. The Bible is clear on this truth, and thinking otherwise just sets us up for disappointment. But it's important to remember that being tempted is not the same as sinning. The craving alone is not what gets us, but rather when we choose to act on it. When we give in, we sin. So how do we stay faithful and receive the crown of life?

As we open the Word each day and spend time in prayer, God supernaturally nourishes our souls. It's there that we find strength and wisdom to stay faithful when the wrong desires and longings creep in. In addition, when we choose to take care of our physical and emotional health by protecting our schedules, pressing PAUSE when life gets too hectic, and making sure we're rested, we will be more alert to the enemy's coaxing. Temptations will come, sometimes screaming and other times like a whisper. But with God and good choices, you'll be able to stand strong in victory.

Dear God, strengthen me to stand strong when I'm tempted to do wrong things. I want the crown of life that comes from obedience. Amen.

GOD'S LOVE NEVER QUITS

You're my God, and I thank you. O my God, I lift high your praise. Thank God—he's so good. His love never quits!
Psalm 118:28-29 MSG

In a world where people often don't hold true to their promises, what a relief to know that God's love never quits. When we make honest mistakes or willful blunders, we're still loved. When we treat others poorly or let our own harsh inner critic beat us down, we're still precious to God. Choosing the wrong path and ending up in a self-made mess doesn't change our worth. Rejecting God's help and trying to figure things out ourselves doesn't change His delight in us. When we place our worth in worldly things, God's compassion for us is unchanging. His love never quits!

If that truth doesn't bring much-needed refreshment to your heart, nothing will. While we live in a very conditional world, we are loved by a very unconditional God. That doesn't mean we can continue living recklessly. But as we pursue righteous living and fall short, it's comforting to know that never changes how the Lord sees us. Let that beautiful truth strengthen you today. Let it bring health to your heart and mind.

Dear God, You are simply amazing. Thank You for loving me no matter what! Amen.

WHEN JOY RETURNS

But let all who take refuge and put their trust in You rejoice,
let them ever sing for joy; because You cover and shelter them,
let those who love Your name be joyful and exult in You.

PSALM 5:11 AMP

There is something so beautiful about realizing we can rest in God. Anytime we're feeling overwhelmed and underwater, let it be a red flag that we're operating in our own strength. It's humanly natural to do, but it's not God's plan. From the beginning, the Lord designed us to need Him desperately. We were made to depend on the Father each day and in every situation, fully and completely. Do you?

If your goal is to be emotionally and spiritually healthy, then taking refuge in God and resting in His presence are essential. Doing these things allows us to take a breath from the craziness of our lives and be restored. We will be able to cease striving and soak in the Lord's invigorating goodness. And slowly but surely, we'll feel joy begin to well up again. Our perception will be aligned with truth. And rather than be overwhelmed by life, we'll be overwhelmed by God's endless compassion.

Dear God, I know that when I find refuge in You, joy will return in abundance because You are its author. Amen.

FOCUSED ON JESUS

Now stay focused on Jesus, who designed and perfected our faith. He endured the cross and ignored the shame of that death because He focused on the joy that was set before Him; and now He is seated beside God on the throne, a place of honor.

HEBREWS 12:2 VOICE

Every day our goal should be to stay focused on Jesus. When we get the difficult phone call that knocks us to our knees, let's keep Him front and center. When we lose our job and face financial ruin, let's look to the Lord above all else. For each heartache and fear, let's stand strong and trust. Let's activate our faith when we're dealing with disappointment. When grief comes, worry sets in, or anxiety springs up, let's keep God as our focal point.

We may feel as if we're all alone, but the reality is that we are not. We have the Holy Spirit's presence with us always, as well as an army of witnesses who have run the race of faith and finished with the Lord as their center of attention. Now it's our turn. So, friend, stand in strength, focused on Jesus, who will bring nourishment to your heart and soul when you need it.

Dear God, let my eyes always rest on You for every need. Amen.

CHOOSING OUR ATTITUDE

Be cheerful no matter what; pray all the time; thank God no matter what happens. This is the way God wants you who belong to Christ Jesus to live.

1 THESSALONIANS 5:16–18 MSG

We get to choose our attitude every day. It's easy to be cheerful when everything is going our way. When relationships are harmonious and finances are flowing and the kids are thriving, optimism comes easily. It's when life hits us in the gut that a positive outlook is harder to come by. This is when we lose our happiness and struggle to stay in a good headspace. This is when our mental and emotional health suffer the most, because without faith, it's hard to regain our balance.

But when we develop a strong connection with God, faith helps us to see the bigger picture. We're able to take a thirty-thousand-foot view of our circumstances in relation to God. And it allows us to see His hand moving in meaningful ways. It affords us an attitude of gratitude, knowing that God always works for our benefit and His glory. So we can trust that God will hold us tight no matter what happens. This beautiful truth is why we can always be in a healthy place—body, mind, and spirit.

Dear God, no matter what, I can have confidence and hope in Your promises to love me and always be with me. Amen.

DESPERATE MOMENTS

If God hadn't been there for me, I never would have made it. The minute I said, "I'm slipping, I'm falling," your love, God, took hold and held me fast. When I was upset and beside myself, you calmed me down and cheered me up.

Psalm 94:17–19 MSG

When the world feels as if it's falling apart, let God's love be your anchor. When it feels like you're slipping and unable to maintain a healthy grip on challenging circumstances, His love will hold you fast. It's true and secure, and it never wavers in changing situations. It's immovable in every way, which allows you to cling to it with confidence. And in a supernatural way, God will bring calm into your heart. He will restore joy and peace so you can catch your breath and regroup your emotions. It's a guarantee you, as a believer, can trust.

Are you struggling today? Are you feeling desperate for help and hope? Are you lacking assurances that you will make it through tough times? Are you overwhelmed mentally and emotionally? If so, ask God to usher you into His presence to find rest for your fatigued soul. He promises to quiet your anxious thoughts.

Dear God, in those desperate moments, remind me that You'll take hold and keep me safe. I trust You to restore peace and joy to me. Amen.

HIS WAYS AND THOUGHTS ARE HIGHER

For just as the heavens are higher than the earth, so are my ways higher than yours, and my thoughts than yours.

ISAIAH 55:9 TLB

Today's verse may feel like a rebuke, but consider that it's also a huge relief and blessing! The fact that God's ways and thoughts are higher than ours lets us know we don't have to figure things out ourselves. We don't always have to know the best path forward. It's not all up to us to fix every problem that arises. Instead, we can rest in God because we trust He has all the answers. Hallelujah!

Too often we stress over details. We get lost in the messy middle and can't see the way out. But God doesn't experience confusion or chaos. He sees the whole situation in its entirety, understanding the causes and cures. His ways and thoughts are inarguably higher! So, sink back into the Lord's embrace and talk to Him. Let God know where you're struggling and ask for guidance. Stop searching for answers within, and ask for His revelation and strength. Ask for rest and wisdom. Ask for comfort and joy restored. The Lord will meet you and bring the clarity you need.

Dear God, thank You for being wiser than humanity! What a huge relief! Amen.

REST AND TRULY TRUST

The Eternal is the source of my strength and the shield that guards me. When I learn to rest and truly trust Him, He sends His help. This is why my heart is singing! I open my mouth to praise Him, and thankfulness rises as song.

PSALM 28:7 VOICE

Too often our hearts grow weary and our bones get tired because we rely on ourselves too much. While we're extraordinary women capable of conquering many giants, we are severely limited by our human condition. And each time we decide to play God in our lives, we are eventually left lacking and exhausted. We aren't designed to navigate this life without the Lord's presence.

Scripture tells us that God is our source! No matter what we need, He's our divine supplier—a promise God takes very seriously. Be it strength, wisdom, hope, peace, joy, perspective, or guidance, when we choose to rest in Him and trust His love, help will arrive. We can lift our voice in praise for His goodness. Because when we ask, He will restore our balance and set us on a healthy path forward.

Dear God, help me choose to rest and truly trust in You to be my source of all good things. I know that when I do, help will come. Thank You for loving me so well! Amen.

NOURISHMENT WILL COME

Those who walk the fields to sow, casting their seed in tears, will one day tread those same long rows, amazed by what's appeared. Those who weep as they walk and plant with sighs will return singing with joy, when they bring home the harvest.

PSALM 126:5–6 VOICE

The above passage is a beautiful reminder that God sees us. He understands the hope we're trying to hold on to behind forced smiles. He knows the depth of our disappointment as we try to keep a positive attitude. When our eyes well up with tears of fear and we keep moving forward regardless, the Lord recognizes our choice to trust. Every day that we get up and cry out for intervention once again, He notices.

Each tear that streams down our cheeks is like a liquid prayer our Father hears with clarity. God is fully aware that our faith has endured the dry seasons where all seems lost. He knows our hearts' greatest desires for ourselves and those we love. And He has seen us sow richly into those desires. Be encouraged by today's passage, recognizing the nourishment that comes to the weary and faithful in God's perfect time.

Dear God, thank You for seeing the daily sowing that comes from my heart. Thank You for knowing the intricacies of what I'm continuing to pray for. And thank You for honoring those who cry out in faith. Amen.

ERUPTING WITH JOY

We live with hope in the Eternal. We wait for Him, for He is our Divine Help and Impenetrable Shield. Our hearts erupt with joy in Him because we trust His holy name. O Eternal, drench us with Your endless love, even now as we wait for You.

PSALM 33:20–22 VOICE

When was the last time your heart erupted with joy? Maybe something came to mind quickly for you, but many people are unable to remember times of joy at all. Life is no cakewalk, especially these days. Relationships are complicated. Finances are touchy. Parenting is challenging. Health is fleeting. And sometimes it seems everyone has gone crazy and circumstances snowball. Chances are, few would argue that point.

But as believers, we can grab on to hope in God. Even when everything hits the fan, we can be certain He will help. Spending time in His Word and praying daily help us become spiritually healthy so we can be confident in our Father's protection. And from that place of trust, we will experience joy erupting from the deepest places. We will feel His overwhelming love, even as we wait to see our deliverance.

Dear God, my only hope to experience any joy in this life is to trust in You with passion and purpose. I'm clinging to You for hope as I wait for Your hand to move. Amen.

PARTNERS WITH JESUS

Dear friends, don't be bewildered or surprised when you go through the fiery trials ahead, for this is no strange, unusual thing that is going to happen to you. Instead, be really glad—because these trials will make you partners with Christ in his suffering, and afterwards you will have the wonderful joy of sharing his glory in that coming day when it will be displayed.

1 PETER 4:12–13 TLB

Today's verse challenges us to think differently. Rather than freak out when hard times happen, we're to see them as opportunities to become more mentally, emotionally, and spiritually healthy. We shouldn't be surprised by messy moments, because the Bible is clear that we all will have trouble in our lives. Everyone will experience hardships. But God wants us to have a shift in perspective, embracing our struggles, knowing that we are partners with Jesus in our suffering.

Let that truth encourage you today. Let it bring peace to your anxious heart. Let it set aflame the light inside that reveals Jesus to others. Let it nurture a weary soul. You have the privilege and burden of sharing in His suffering.

Dear God, what an honor to partner with Jesus in any way. Forgive me for not seeing the bigger picture of suffering like I do now. The next time those seasons come, give me an eternal perspective so I can see the goodness in them. Amen.

WHAT SATISFIES A HUNGRY SOUL

Your words are what sustain me; they are food to my hungry soul. They bring joy to my sorrowing heart and delight me. How proud I am to bear your name, O Lord.

JEREMIAH 15:16 TLB

Nothing will sustain the spiritual health of a believer like God's Word. Following Jesus creates a hunger to learn more and understand more, and scripture is the food that always satisfies. It strengthens us so we're able to withstand the storms of life. It encourages us to trust God's timing. It reminds us of who He is and what He promises for the believer. The Bible offers a new way of seeing life, a divine perspective that only it can offer. And it releases the gift of joy.

Are you spending time in God's Word daily? If so, can you see the way it has blessed you? If not, what's keeping you from digging in? Time in the Word is the most important meal of the day because it helps set the tone for your heart and mind. Without it, a believer risks living in defeat and discouragement. The choice is yours to make every day, friend. Choose wisely.

Dear God, create in me a hunger for more of Your Word, knowing it's what will sustain me as I walk through this life. Amen.

GOD KNOWS WHAT HE'S DOING

"I know what I'm doing. I have it all planned out—plans to take care of you, not abandon you, plans to give you the future you hope for."

JEREMIAH 29:11 MSG

Worry about an unknown future can wreck our emotional balance. Tremendous fear can overtake us as we look ahead, predicting only terrible outcomes. As we obsess about the future, that unmanaged anxiety can rob us of peace and joy in the here and now. And in most cases, what we worry about the most never comes to pass. It merely disrupts our hearts and minds and leaves us mentally bankrupt.

If you struggle in this way, be encouraged by today's verse. Let it settle your spirit as you recognize that God has everything under control. Circumstances may feel chaotic, but He is aware of all that's happening. He has planned every detail and has full knowledge of the past, present, and future. God knows what He is doing and has made provision for your future. Even more, we can find comfort by understanding that His plans are to care for you with compassion and purpose. He will never leave you alone to figure things out for yourself. Today, friend, rest in the beautiful truth from Jeremiah.

Dear God, calm my anxious heart with reminders that You know what You're doing and I can rest in that truth. Thank You for taking care of me today and forever. Amen.

THE DESIRE TO BE KNOWN

"Then you will call on Me and you will come and pray to Me, and I will hear [your voice] and I will listen to you. Then [with a deep longing] you will seek Me and require Me [as a vital necessity] and [you will] find Me when you search for Me with all your heart."

JEREMIAH 29:12–13 AMP

As women, we have a huge desire to be known. We want to be seen and understood at the core because being seen and known promotes a healthy emotional balance. It makes us feel validated. We feel accepted and loved. And it's a powerful way to encourage a weary soul and burdened heart.

Consider that God wants the same from us. Of course, not for the same reasons. He doesn't struggle with insecurity or need validation from His own creation. But God wants us to seek Him with a deep longing and with all our hearts. The Lord wants us to cry out to Him with great passion because we know His ability to save and restore. And when we do, God promises that we will find Him. He will show up and meet our needs in the perfect way and at the perfect time.

Dear God, hear me cry out for Your help.
Know that I am seeking You with fervor.
Let me feel Your presence right now. Amen.

SCRIPTURE INDEX

OLD TESTAMENT

Exodus
14:13–14 141
33:14–15 144

1 Chronicles
16:10-12 156

Psalms
4:8 147
5:11 176
16:11 166
23:1–3 51
23:4 54
23:5 59
23:6 56
28:7 181
30:2–3 168
30:10–11 170
33:20–22 183
37:7 148
46:10 149
61:1–3 142
62:1–2 153
71:15–16 172
73:26 154
90:12 133
91:1–2 152
94:17–19 179
118:21 171
118:28-29 175
119:105–106 160
126:5–6 182
127:2 145
139:13–14 46
139:23–24 49
143:8 137

Proverbs
3:1–2 68
3:5–6 40
3:7–8 41
3:9–10 42
3:11–12 44
3:21–22 74
3:24–26 150
3:25–26 82
3:30–31 91
16:9 130
17:9 119
17:14 124
17:22 116
19:21 139
21:5 136
31:30 143

Isaiah
26:3 138
40:31 158
55:9 180
58:11 50

Jeremiah
15:16 185
29:11 186
29:12–13 187
31:25 151

Daniel

1:8 89

Zephaniah

3:17 157

NEW TESTAMENT

Matthew

6:3–4 107
6:7–8 100
6:16 92
6:19–21 79
6:24 86
6:26–27 61
6:31–33 27
6:34 29
11:28–30 114
22:37 88

Mark

6:31–32 104
6:41–42 106
12:29–30 33
12:31 .... 34, 35
12:33 37

Luke

1:37 155
12:5–6 113
12:7 115
12:11–12 118
12:15 121
12:22, 24 123
12:25–26 128
12:30–31 134
12:33–34 140
12:39–40 146

John

1:14 163
6:63–64 164
10:10 102
14:16–17 81
14:23 84
14:27 87
15:10–11 167
15:18–19 173
17:17–18 161

Romans

12:1 20
12:2 23
12:3 24
12:7–8 26
12:9 28
12:10 34
12:11 39
12:12–13 48
12:14 53
12:15 57
12:16 60
12:17 65
12:18 72
12:19 77
12:21 83

1 Corinthians

3:3 101
3:16–17 12
3:18 103

6:19–20 9
10:13 31
10:23 36
10:24 43
10:31 32
12:24–27 38

2 Corinthians

9:7 76
9:8–9 80

Galatians

2:20 75
6:1 18
6:2–3 19
6:4–5 22
6:7–8 21
6:9 135
6:9–10 25
6:14 30

Ephesians

2:8–9 94
2:10 96
2:13 98
2:19 99
4:2–3 64
4:17–18 67
4:22–24 69
4:25 71
4:26–27 78
4:29 85
4:31–32 70
5:2 45
5:3–4 47
5:8–9 52
5:10–11 58
5:15–17 .... 66, 132
5:19–20 73

Philippians

2:3–4 90
2:12–13 93
2:14–15 95
2:20–21 97
4:2 13
4:4–5 14
4:6–7 11
4:8 15
4:12–13 16
4:19 17

Colossians

3:16 162

1 Thessalonians

5:16–18 178
5:23–24 159

1 Timothy

4:7–8 109
4:12 111

2 Timothy

1:5 105
1:6–7 108
1:9 110
1:12 112

Hebrews

4:9–11 10
12:1 126
12:2 177
12:3 127
12:7–8 129
12:14–15 131

James

1:2–4 169
1:12 174
1:21 165
5:9 55
5:12 62
5:16 63

1 Peter

4:12–13 184
5:7 122
5:8 120
5:10 125

1 John

1:8–9 117

3 John

2 8

DEVOTIONS FOR YOUR LOVELY HEART

God's love covers every area of our lives—from the good times to the heartbreaking times, He cares about it all! This lovely book includes devotions and prayer starters to help make your faith stronger, deeper, and more fully rooted in an all-important relationship with your gracious and powerful provider—God. Prayer changes things, and here you'll find true refreshment for your spirit and a renewed sense of God's loving presence in everyday life.

Flexible Casebound / 979-8-89151-232-0